Berlitz

Costa Blanca

Front cover: The beach at Calpe

Right: The castle at Sax

TOP 10 ATTRACTIONS

Peñón de Ifach • The dramatic rock at Calpe is rich in plant and birdlife *(page 46)*

City of Arts and Sciences This futuristic cultural complex is the toast of Valencia *(page 56)*

Benidorm • Spain's perennially popular resort has all a holidaymaker could need *(page 36)*

Orihuela • This city has a particularly rich architect heritage *(page 64)*

tillo de Santa Bárbara • Perched above Alicante, the ion's capital, the old castle offers superb views *(page 26)*

Murcia Cathedral • Where the baroque and Gothic rub shoulders *(page 72)*

tagena • The 'City of stles' – you'll see one on rly every hill around this port *(page 68)*

Guadalest • Built by the Moors over a thousand years ago, this village occupies a dramatic rocky position *(page 41)*

Mar Menor • The 'Lesser ' has calm, warm waters, king it a natural swimming ol *(page 66)*

The palm groves of Elche • Nurtured by the Moors, the palms that surround the town form a World Heritage Site *(page 61)*

80

50

78

CONTENTS

Features

28

40

99

INTRODUCTION

A thousand years ago, the Moors thought that the Costa Blanca was a paradise, a fragment from the next world that had fortuitously fallen onto this one. They had a point. For 10 months of the year, a blazing sun warms beaches, ochre plains and misty, wind-sculpted mountains. Olive, eucalyptus and carob trees dot ancient fields. Orange groves fill the valleys and, in January and February, the mountains burst into colour with pink-and-white almond blossoms.

Spain's fabulous 'White Coast' was christened nearly 2,000 years before the arrival of the Moors by Greek traders, who founded the colony of Akra Leuka (White Headland) on a site near today's Alicante, the main town on the coast. The Romans called the provincial capital Lucentum, City of Light, the Moors called it al-Laqant, and today the letters 'AL' and 'LA' (Lucentum Alicante) are significantly displayed on Alicante's crest.

The Tourists Arrive

The exceptional tourist potential of the Costa Blanca's sun, sea and mountains remained unexploited until the early 1960s, when *alicantinos* looked north to the growing popularity of the Costa Brava and south to the Costa del Sol and realised that they could offer something just as good, if not even

The beach at Benidorm

Adjust your clock

Life in Spain is out of synch with the rest of Europe and the best thing to do is adapt to the local rhythm rather than fight against it. The morning *(mañana)* lasts until around 1.30 or 2pm (midday here is around 3pm) and all offices, shops and museums only reopen at 5pm when the afternoon *(tarde)* begins.

better. *El boom*, as the local people call it, was inevitable. Benidorm, a small fishing village with a sublime coast, rapidly took off and today it has scores of hotels – including the tallest in Spain – and hundreds of apartments and villas to accommodate nearly 200,000 summer holidaymakers a day, on top of the 65,000 residents. A four-lane motorway (with minor interruptions) follows the coast from the French frontier as far as Alicante and thereafter continues south inland towards the Costa del Sol, and every year several million tourists speed along it to the resorts. The region is served by Alicante airport, just outside the city, and regular ferries operate from Alicante and Denia to the Balearic islands.

Two Costas

Merely defining the coasts of Spain calls for a word about contemporary Spanish government. The organisation and promotion of tourism is the responsibility of the *comunidades autónomas* (autonomous communities). Although the term 'Costa Blanca' is sometimes loosely applied to Spain's southeast coast, it is officially the coast of the province of Alicante, stretching precisely from Denia in the

Wildlife Havens

Several nature reserves are within easy reach of the resorts. The Peñón de Ifach at Calpe *(see page 46)* is the most conspicuous – a crag that towers over the sea. Another coastal peak is Mount Montgó *(see page 49)* between Denia and Jávea, of particular interest to botanists. South of Alicante are the glassy salt pans of Santa Pola and Torrevieja *(see page 58)*, which have rich populations of birds, including flamingoes. The Mar Menor *(see page 66)* is also good for birdwatching. Inland, Font Roja Nature Reserve *(see page 32)* near Alcoy is home to well-preserved kermes oak woodland and a rich variety of fauna and flora.

north to Pilar de la Horadada in the south. The province of Alicante forms part of the *comunidad* of Valencia, which has its capital in the north at Valencia, Spain's third largest city and also included in this guide. Across the southern border is the quite separate *comunidad* of Murcia whose coast (which includes the Mar Menor and runs as far as Aguilas on the border with Andalucía) is known as the Costa Cálida. In practice, this only matters when asking for information, as each region takes care of itself and will tell you little about its neighbour.

Kitesurfing in the Mar Menor

Between them, the coasts of Alicante and Murcia offer extremely varied landscapes, from broad sandy beaches to intimate coves, from lush wetlands to arid badlands, from the tower blocks of Benidorm to attractive low-rise towns like Jávea. Inland there are winding country roads that climb hillsides first terraced by the Moors, serving picturesque villages unchanged for centuries. Perhaps the most impressive excursion inland is Guadalest, north of Benidorm, where a dramatically situated Moorish fortress is entered through a thousand-year-old tunnel. Another favourite excursion is to Elche where thousands of palm trees, thought to have been planted by the Carthaginians, form Europe's largest date-palm forest, designated a UNESCO World Heritage Site.

Historic Játiva, the 'city of a thousand fountains'

Art and Architecture

The region's cultural heritage includes some fine art and architecture, starting with the exceptional Bronze Age gold artefacts on display in Villena. Examples of Francisco Salzillo's Baroque polychrome wood sculpture are to be found in almost every church in his native province of Murcia, and the exquisite processional figures carved by the modern Valencian sculptor, Mariano Benlliure, bring many visitors to the village of Crevillente at Easter.

The two regional capitals, Valencia to the north and Murcia to the south, are both lively university cities with fine cathedrals and many excellent museums. Of particular note is Valencia's Museo de Bellas Artes which houses 14th- and 15th-century Valencian art, as well as works by Bosch, El Greco, Velázquez and Goya. The fascinating (and visually stunning) City of Arts and Sciences in Valencia is the Costa's answer to the Guggenheim.

Fun and Fiestas

Entertainment for everyone is within easy reach on the Costa Blanca including some fabulous clubs and a wide variety of sports, such as water-skiing, windsurfing, kite-surfing, scuba-diving, tennis and golf. You can see top matadors fight in *corridas* in the major towns or, preferable for some, visit a safari park where giraffes roam free in the Spanish wilds. The bullrings of Alicante and Benidorm are also used for major concerts and sporting events.

Spain is celebrated for its fiestas *(see page 89)*, and one of the most spectacular is Alcoy's 'Moors and Christians' extravaganza with its re-enacting of old rivalries. Even more dramatic are Las Fallas in Valencia, in March (St Joseph's Day), and Alicante's Hogueras de San Juan in June, in which giant effigies are burned at midnight, a legacy from a pagan mid-summer sacrifice to the fire gods.

Produce and People

Although tourism is the major industry in this region, agriculture continues to thrive on reliable underground water supplies, and age-old crafts continue to flourish. Paper, shoes, toys and dolls are profitable exports, and lace, cane and *esparto* grass-work are important cottage industries. At Jijona, factories continue to make *turrón* – a honey-and-almond sweet – in much the same way as the Moors once did *(see page 31)*. Torrevieja's ancient salt industry remains one of Europe's largest *(see page 58)*.

Many people in Valencia and Alicante speak *valenciano*, a dialect of Catalán, which makes Alicante 'Alicant'. This language can be seen on street and road signs. But everyone also speaks Castilian, the official language of Spain, which is used in this book. Learn a few words and phrases and doors will open to you.

Festive local girl

A BRIEF HISTORY

Nothing has had a greater impact on the Costa Blanca than foreign invasion: Iberians, Phoenicians, Greeks, Romans, Visigoths and Moors all moulded Spain's Mediterranean shores centuries before international tourism gained a foothold. Before all of these were the first inhabitants: Neanderthal men, who lived primitively and spent a large part of their time hunting. Then, as the Stone Age came to an end, short dark-skinned Iberians started to make their way from North Africa to the Spanish Peninsula. These fierce fighters skilled in guerrilla warfare roamed the Mediterranean foothills, painting a vivid record of their battles on the walls of their rock shelters.

Early Traders

The Phoenicians ventured across the Mediterranean from present-day Lebanon, reaching Spain by about 1100BC. They founded many trading settlements in the 'remote' or 'hidden land' that they named *Span* or *Spania*, and among the many on the Costa Blanca were Elche and Játiva.

After about 650BC, Greek traders arrived to compete for Spain's rich mineral deposits and fertile land. Their influence was short-lived, although the olive and the grape, Greek legacies, are still cultivated in the region.

The Carthaginians, a people related to the Phoenicians, came from North Africa and subsequently took over much of southern Spain, beginning with Cádiz in 501BC. The town had sought help from

Elche's stone lady

The Lady of Elche (La Dama de Elche), a stone bust found near Elche and dating from the 4th century BC, is one of Spain's greatest archaeological treasures. Nobody is sure who the figure was or if its creator was Iberian or Greek.

the Carthaginian army in its war against local tribes, and the 'invited guest' decided to stay. The main centre of Carthaginian power in Spain was located on the Costa Blanca: Carthago Nova, now Cartagena, followed in prominence by Alicante.

In 218BC Hannibal, the Carthaginian general, led one of history's greatest military marches up the Spanish coast and across southern France to Italy, crossing the Pyrenees and the Alps, in the hope of surprising an unsuspecting Rome. The Romans responded by invading Spain to cut off Hannibal's supply route and staying there for around 600 years.

Lady of Elche replica in the Huerto del Cura *(see page 61)*

Under Roman Rule

It took the Romans almost 300 years to subdue the Iberian tribes, and Rome's influence on the country through its engineering and architecture was significant. Stability and unity were promoted by the introduction of Latin, from which modern Spanish developed, and Roman law is still the basis of Spain's legal system. When the Roman empire crumbled, the country was overrun by various northern tribes. Visigoths, Christian peoples who had lived under Roman law in southern France, eventually held much of southern Spain under their control which they maintained for some 300 years.

Moorish Domination

In AD711, less than a century after the death of the prophet Mohammed, General Tariq Ibn Ziyad landed at Gibraltar with 12,000 Berber troops. Within 10 years the Moors' green-crescent standard flew over most of Spain and the occupation would last 800 years. It was from the Moors that a number of towns in the region – Kartajanah (Cartagena), Mursiyah (Murcia) and Xàtiva (Játiva) – got their names.

The Moors taxed non-believers rather than trying to convert them, and designed much of the landscape seen today. They introduced the manufacture of paper, which is carried on today in Játiva. They laid out a system of irrigation still in use in the Guadalest Valley and filled the *huertas* (orchards) of the Costa Blanca with oranges, peaches and pomegranates. Rice, cotton and sugar cane were also first cultivated on Spanish soil by the Moors.

Numerous Moorish fortifications on the Costa Blanca survive, and the pottery of the region reflects the influence of Moorish craftsmen. Learning was considerably advanced by the Moors, and a medical treatise written by an Arab

The Moors' Legacy

The Muslim rulers of Spain may have been driven out centuries ago but they left behind them an indelible legacy. Everywhere along the Costa Blanca you can still see hillsides meticulously carved into terraces, as well as lush fields and orchards near the coast which are fed by the Moors' ingenious system of irrigation channels. Many surviving castles are the remains of Arab fortresses and the tortuous street patterns of almost all the old villages and towns preserve an undeniable oriental flavour. Alicante province's favourite traditional celebrations, meanwhile, are the parades and mock battles of the Moors and Christians. The Moors may be long gone but they haven't been forgotten.

physician in Crevillente is recognised as revolutionary for its time.

Feeling the rising strength of Christianity, and weakened by fighting among themselves, the Moors sought outside help from the Almohades. From what is now Morocco, these Berber warriors quickly reduced Moorish Spain to a province of their North African empire, endowing it with enough strength to resist the Christian forces a while longer.

El Cid takes Valencia from the Moors in 1094

The Tide Turns

Fortunes swayed to and fro for centuries, but it was not until 1212, at Las Navas de Tolosa in southern Spain, that the Christians gained their first decisive victory. The Christian kingdoms of the north gradually captured and annexed former bastions of Moorish rule: Ferdinand III conquered Murcia for Castile in 1242; Denia and Játiva fell to James the Conqueror of Catalonia-Aragon in 1244, and in 1265 he finally secured Cartagena. The Moors were on the retreat, withdrawing to Granada, where they held out until 1492.

The Golden Age

Spain's golden century began under the 'Catholic Monarchs', a title conferred by Pope Alexander VI on Ferdinand II and Isabella, who united the country under the Christian king-

Map of the region, 1500s

doms of Aragón and Castile shortly before the fall of Granada. That same eventful year, Columbus, seeking a western route to the East on behalf of the Catholic Monarchs, arrived in the Americas. And Ferdinand and Isabella consolidated Christian rule by decreeing that all Jews – the banking and business experts – must adopt Catholicism or be exiled. The Moors – a source of cheap labour and vital agricultural know-how – were given the same ultimatum in 1502.

The Segura Valley was the last part of Spain to be inhabited by Muslims, who abandoned their fortresses there in 1505. As the Inquisition established its reign of terror to stamp out heresy, converted Jews *(conversos)* and Muslims *(moriscos)* were looked upon with suspicion, and many left the country or were condemned to death. Agricultural productivity suffered considerably after the official expulsion of the *moriscos* in 1609.

The conquest of the New World brought Spain fame and immense wealth, especially under Charles I and Philip II, and though the Golden Age brought prosperity to Alicante as a major Mediterranean port, exporting wine, olive oil, rice and wool, it was the Atlantic ports of Seville and Cádiz that prospered most. Much of the New World gold was simply squandered and wasted, and decline set in. In 1588 the ill-prepared

Armada set out to invade England, only to be beaten by the English and Dutch navies and a providential storm. Another important defeat took place at Rocroi, in Flanders, in 1643, when the French routed Spanish troops, causing them to withdraw from northern Europe.

French Ascendancy

Spanish internal affairs became the concern of other great powers after Charles II died in 1700 without an heir. The Archduke Charles of Austria competed with France's Philip of Bourbon for the Spanish throne in the ensuing War of the Spanish Succession. Murcia was defended from the invasion of Archduke Charles by its bishop, with the help of local people; Játiva fought the succession of Philip so fiercely that when resistance was finally overcome in 1707, the town's name was changed to San Felipe. The former name was not restored until the 19th century. Philip finally gained the Spanish throne in 1713.

Nearly 100 years later, during the Napoleonic wars, Spanish ships fought alongside the French fleet against Lord Nelson at Cape Trafalgar, southeast of Cádiz. But as the wars continued, Napoleon, distrustful of his ally, forced the Spanish king to abdicate in 1808 and imposed his brother Joseph as king of Spain. He sent thousands of troops across the Pyrenees to subdue the Spaniards, who then revolted. Aided by British troops, the Spanish drove the French out of the Iberian peninsula. Denia, held by the enemy, was blockaded for eight months in 1813. The

Játiva's revenge

Philip V might have put Játiva to the torch for backing his opponent in the War of the Spanish Succession, but the town has been getting the last laugh on him ever since. In the Museo Municpal a full-length portrait of the haughty monarch hangs upside down.

18th-century *azulejas* – glazed tiles

Peninsular War (1808–14) is referred to in Spain as the War of Independence, and the country's first, though short-lived, constitution was drafted during this period.

From Decline to Chaos

Hopes of setting up a constitutional monarchy were quickly dashed and Spain was plunged into a century of power struggles at home. Overseas, her American colonies revolted and gained independence. Soon there was little left of the once great Spanish empire, and an attempt in 1873 to form a republic failed. In 1902, Alfonso XIII became king at the age of 16. His reign was a difficult time for Spain; prosperity and stability eluded the country, which remained neutral during World War I. In 1923, assailed by economic problems and with catastrophe imminent, the king accepted a general, Miguel Primo de Rivera, as dictator. Just six years later the opposition of radical forces resulted in Primo de Rivera's fall.

Neither reform nor the maintenance of order seemed possible. In 1931 the king went into exile following anti-royalist election results, and another republic was founded.

Parliamentary democracy was impeded by the ideological commitment of various political factions and compromise was rare. Spain floundered in a sea of political strikes and violence. Then the Left won the 1936 elections and was immediately in violent collision with the Right. In July 1936 a large section of the army under General Francisco Franco rose in revolt against the government. On Franco's side were monarchists, conservatives, the Church and the right-wing Falangists. Against him were republicans, liberals, socialists, communists and anarchists. The ensuing Civil War became one of the great ideological battlegrounds of the 20th century. Fascist Germany and Italy supplied Franco's Nationalists with arms and air power, and the Soviet Union initially gave aid to Spain's communists. The bloodshed lasted for three years and cost hundreds of thousands of lives.

Even after the war, the hardship continued. But despite pressure from Hitler, Franco, who emerged as Spain's new *caudillo* (leader), managed to keep his exhausted country out of World War II.

During the years of postwar reconstruction, Franco, although a tyrant, encouraged tourism on a grand scale as a way to bring currency into the country. This policy profoundly affected the economy and the people, and transformed Spain's most attractive coasts, not always for the better.

Tourism booms

The first real tourist boom took place in the 1960s: skyscrapers replaced the old *ventas* (inns) and the number of visitors to Alicante province shot up to over three million a year. Smaller but significant booms followed in the 1970s and 1980s, spreading down the coast to the Mar Menor and inland to the valleys and sierras.

Benidorm in 1963, before *el boom*

Modern Times

When Franco died in 1975, Prince Juan Carlos, the grandson of the Bourbon King Alfonso XIII, succeeded to the Spanish throne and led the transition from totalitarianism to democracy. In 1978 a new constitution was introduced, granting wide-ranging powers to the regions. In 1986 Spain joined the European Economic Community (EEC), bringing much-needed funds into the country, and in 2002 Spain became one of the 12 European Union countries to adopt the euro.

Although autonomy had been granted to the regions, further powers continued to be sought by the more vociferous areas, particularly Catalonia and the Basque country. In 2003 the Basque terrorist organisation ETA detonated bombs in Alicante and Benidorm, and several people were injured.

Spain has emerged as a major player on the world stage. Conservative prime minister José María Aznar joined George Bush and Tony Blair in talks on the eve of the invasion of Iraq in 2003. In March 2004 a lethal terrorist bomb attack on trains approaching Madrid's Atocha station was organised by Islamic terrorists, killing 191 people. In the general election three days later the Socialists were returned to power under Rodriguez Zapatero.

Historical Landmarks

2000BC Phoenicians establish settlement near Orihuela.
223BC Founding of Cartagena by the Carthaginians.
219–18BC Roman subjugation of the Iberian peninsula.
AD711 Moorish conquest of Spain.
1036 Denia becomes capital of Moorish Kingdom.
1223–43 Murcia becomes an independent kingdom under the Almohades.
1246 Alicante reconquered for the Christians by Alfonso X of Castile.
1296 Murcia transferred to the Crown of Aragon, coming under Castile eight years later.
1308 Alicante incorporated into the Kingdom of Valencia.
1490 Alicante officially declared a city.
1492 End of the reconquest of Spain.
1609 Expulsion of the *moriscos* (Moorish converts to Christianity).
1691 French bombardment of Alicante lasts seven days.
1702–14 War of the Spanish Succession; Alicante bombarded by British navy, destroying castle of Santa Bárbara.
1804–14 War of Independence (Peninsular War); Valencia is occupied by the French, and Alicante becomes capital of Province of Valencia.
1829 Earthquake in Murcia; 6,000 die.
1838 Murcia becomes capital of its province.
1858 Alicante connected to central Spain by railway.
1873 Cartagena briefly declares independence from Spanish Republic.
1897 La Dama de Elche, from 4th century BC, discovered at La Alcudia.
1912 University of Murcia founded.
1936–9 Spanish Civil War. Alicante is one of the last cities to fall.
1963 Discovery of the treasure of Villena.
1967 Alicante airport (El Altet) opens.
1975 Death of Franco.
1979 University of Alicante founded.
1982 Autonomous communities of Murcia and Alicante created.
2002 Spain adopts the euro.
2004 Valencia's City of Arts and Sciences completed.

FAETON
24

WHERE TO GO

With such a long stretch of coast to cover and so many historic towns to visit inland, the Costa Blanca may seem difficult to navigate – particularly if you don't have a car. But the itineraries in the following pages take in all the sights worth seeing in this sprawling region, and every one of these places of interest can be reached by public transport.

Most visitors stay within easy reach of Alicante, so we begin here. At the centre of the region's road network, Alicante is also a logical base for motorists and for train and bus connections. Benidorm is another destination for many tourists, and this popular resort provides another good point of departure for excursions up and down the coast, as well as to picturesque villages, especially Guadalest, in the interior.

In striking distance to the north of the Costa Blanca is Valencia, one of Spain's most attractive and dynamic cities. To the south of Alicante is the province of Murcia, which has three historic cities and a host of smaller sights. Its coast, the Costa Cálida, served by Murcia-San Javier Airport on the north shore of the Mar Menor, is slightly less developed than the Costa Blanca, but also has its share of cultural sights and beauty spots.

ALICANTE

Swaying palms and luminous skies, along with some of Spain's best restaurants and tapas bars, lure visitors to the provincial capital of Alicante (Alacant). It is both a busy functional city and a holiday resort that is as popular with European holidaymakers today as it was with Greek and Roman colonisers in ancient times. You'll always see cosmopolitan crowds here,

The Peñón de Ifach, Costa Blanca's most distinctive landmark

especially on the **Explanada de España**, the splendid promenade that stretches alongside the harbour, paved with a wave mosaic made from six million pebbles. You can stroll to the music of a band on Sundays or try one of the restaurants on the Paseo. Just east of the Explanada, an irresistible stretch of sandy beach, the **Playa del Postiguet**, beckons.

City Sights

The broad **Rambla de Méndez Núñez**, running at right angles to the Explanada, is good for a morning's shopping and has a lively market at one end. It's also the route taken by civic and religious processions, notably the Hogueras de San Juan parade held every June. Off the *rambla* (a broad tree-lined avenue) to the right is the Calle Mayor, a pedestrianised street. Here, street vendors hawk pens, watches and jewellery, and on religious holidays processions pass by on their way from the **Catedral de San Nicolás de Bari**. Situated a stone's throw from the Calle Mayor on Plaza Abad Penalva in the old town, the cathedral was considerably restored after the Civil War. Note the impressive nave and façade, excellent examples of the austere style of Juan de Herrera (1530–97), who also designed the Escorial Palace near Madrid.

The nave of the Catedral de San Nicolás de Bari

Walk beyond the Calle Mayor and the tranquil Plaza de Santa Faz to get to the Plaza del Ayuntamiento, where there's a coin and stamp market on Sundays and public holidays. The square is the site of the **Ayuntamiento** (Town Hall; open Mon–Fri 9am–2pm, Sat

Alicante's Explanada de España

9am–1pm), with a stunning twin-towered baroque façade designed in the 18th century by Lorenzo Chápuli, a local architect. A highly polished brass stud on the first step of the main staircase registers a height exactly 3m (10ft) above sea level. This is Spain's official altitude-measuring point. The handsome, red-lettered marble plaque on the same staircase is a copy of the city's charter, presented by Ferdinand II of Aragón in 1490.

The Ayuntamiento houses a small picture gallery and a chapel with tiles from Manises, an important Valencian ceramics centre. Look for the painting of Saint Nicholas of Bari, the patron saint of Alicante, over the altar. There are 18th-century royal portraits in the **Salón Azul** (Blue Room) and archives that preserve the document of privileges granted to the city by Alfonso X, the Wise, in the 13th century.

A short distance uphill brings you to the Plaza Santa María and the magnificent baroque **Iglesia de Santa María**. The church dates from the 14th century and is one of many built

Summer Festival

Alicante's Summer Festival, in July and August, of music, dance and theatre, attracts top names. It is held in the Paseo del Puerto.

during the Christianisation of territory won from the Moors by James I in legendary 13th-century battles; it stands on the site of a former mosque. Works by Chagall, Braque, Dalí, Picasso and many other 20th-century artists hang next door in the **Museo de la Asegurada** (closed temporarily, but usually open Tues–Sat 10am–2pm and 5–9pm, 4–8pm in winter, Sun 10.30am–2.30pm; admission fee). This museum also includes the impressive collection of local artist Eusebio Sempere, whose 1978 star-shaped metal sculpture stands in Plaça Portal d'Elx.

Beyond the Plaza Santa María you'll find the tiny **Barrio de Santa Cruz**. This quarter is all that remains of the Villa Vieja, or old town. You can still see fascinating glimpses of traditional narrow streets, where houses are decorated with potted plants and wrought-iron grilles.

Castles

From this *barrio* you'll be able to see the most prominent sight in Alicante, the historic **Castillo de Santa Bárbara** (open daily 10am–8pm; admission fee), perched 115m (380ft) above the city on Mount Benacantil. The site has been fortified since prehistoric times and offers beautiful views on a clear day of the Sierra de Aitana, San Juan, Santa Pola, Benidorm, and the Tabarca islands in the distance.

To get to the castle, drive up the winding road to the summit or use the lift at the far end of Calle Juan Bautista Lafora, opposite the Postiguet beach. Santa Bárbara, built by the Carthaginians in the 3rd century BC, was so well fortified that for nearly two thousand years nobody conquered it. While there, visit the **Collección Capa**, a display of contemporary Spanish sculpture, including Salvador Dalí's *Newton*.

On the opposite side of town, in the Barrio San Blas, is the smaller **Castillo de San Fernando**, begun during the War of Independence (1808–14). The castle, set above the trees of the small **Parque Municipal**, provides a favourite spot for viewing Santa Bárbara and the port in the late afternoon.

The **Museo Arqueológico Provincial** (open winter Tues–Sat 10am–7pm, Sun 10am–2pm, summer Tues–Sat 11am–2pm and 6pm–midnight, Sun 11am–2pm; admission fee), housed in the former Hospital de San Juan de Díos on Plaza Doctor Gómez Ulla, contains an interesting ceramics collection, with some pieces dating back to the Greeks. Take a look at the graceful pottery of the Iberians, adorned with simple painted lines, and the Stone Age finds, including pottery and bone bracelets. There are also fascinating Carthaginian and Greek carvings and Moorish relics. The museum building itself is magnificent.

The view from Castillo de Santa Bárbara

Alicante's Beaches

Fine sandy beaches have made Alicante not only the administrative and transport hub of the Costa Blanca but a major resort in its own right. You can easily walk to the closest beaches but, if you want to go further, a scenic narrow-gauge railway, known as 'El Tram' *(see page 123)*, departs from Alicante for beaches further away, sticking close to the sand for the first 10km (6 miles) of its trajectory and ultimately reaching Denia *(see page 49)*.

The best of Alicante's beaches are north of the centre. The handiest is the urban beach of **Playa del Postiguet**, backed by palm trees. Tacked onto this, next to the narrow-gauge train station, is the **Playa del Cocó**, where fishermen used to haul their boats out of the water. A little further away is the **Playa de la Albufereta** beside the site of the Roman-Iberian settlement of Lucentum out of which the modern city

On the beach at Alicante

eventually grew. Adjacent is a small beach, the **Playa de la Almadrada**, mostly used by local residents. The coast then bends round a small headland topped by a lighthouse and pockmarked by the coves of Cala de los Judíos, Cala de los Cantarales and Cala Palmera, the last two popular for nude sunbathing because of their seclusion.

On the other side of the headland is Alicante's favourite beach, the **Playa de San Juan**. Built up and usually busy with life, it stretches for 7km (5 miles) and has almost every facility you could ask for, including showers, lifeguards, playgrounds, pedal-boat hire and volleyball nets. It's also renowned for its countless restaurants specialising in rice and fish dishes and for its nightlife.

Going south from the centre of Alicante towards the airport is the relatively low-key **Playa de El Saladar** (also known as Playa de Urbanova). With views back over the city and its bay, it is not only a good place to flop on the sand but also a pleasant strip to stroll along at sunset.

Santa Faz Monastery

Outside town, on the main Valencia road, the **Monasterio de la Santa Faz** attracts thousands of devotees during the annual May celebration of the Santa Faz (Holy Face). Armed with canes decorated with bunches of rosemary, the participants proceed on foot to the monastery, where they venerate the Holy Face cloth. According to tradition, the cloth retained the bloodstained image of Jesus' face after Saint Veronica used it to wipe his brow as he went on his way to Calvary. The sacred relic was first worshipped in the Alicante region during a drought in 1489. As it was being carried across the site of the present-day monastery, the Santa Faz is said to have suddenly become too heavy to hold, and believers claim that a tear fell from the right eye of the image. This was interpreted as a sign to construct

A cove on Tabarca

the building that has housed the cloth ever since. The Santa Faz can be seen at the high altar or in a chapel off the sacristy.

According to Roman Catholic authorities, the original cloth was divided into three. The other two pieces are kept in Jaén, also in Spain, and in the Vatican.

Tabarca

The small, flat island of **Tabarca** lies about an hour by boat from Alicante and half an hour from Santa Pola. You won't see any pirates here, as the last of them sailed away from their former stronghold in 1786. But you will find fishermen, many of whom are direct descendants of the 600 or so Genoese mercenaries King Charles III rescued from captivity on Tunisia's Tabarka Island (hence the name). It was tourism that finally saved the declining population from fading away altogether, and provided islanders with a priest and teacher at last. One enterprising islander, Angel Ruiz, has set up a **Museum of Miniature Paintings** in his home, with copies of masterpieces painted on pebbles.

Sun-seeking visitors, mostly Spaniards, flock to the island on Sundays, the most popular day for excursions. Even then, you'll always be able to find peace and quiet on one of the tiny seaweed-draped coves beyond the main sandy bay.

INLAND FROM ALICANTE

For a change of scenery, drive north of Alicante into the rocky lunar landscape of the Cabeço d'Or mountains. This is where you'll find the **Cuevas de Canalobre** (open daily July–Sept and Easter week 10.30am–7.50pm, Oct–June 11.30am–5.30pm) at an altitude of 700m (2,300ft). They are reached by following the N-340 from San Juan de Alicante until the turn-off for **Busot**, where signs mark the way. The caves were known to the Moors and used for cold storage. Floodlights are used to dramatise the eerie ranks of gigantic stalagmites and stalactites, populating the chambers that rise to heights of up to 115m (380ft). The acoustics are so exceptional that summer concerts are held in the caves.

Turrón

Turrón, Spain's favourite Christmas sweet, comes in many varieties, but the two traditional ones are *turrón de Alicante*, a hard nougat, and *turrón de Jijona*, which is soft and moist. The content of *turrón* produced in the province of Alicante is monitored by a regulatory body to ensure that it has just the right amount of almonds and honey.

Jijona

Jijona (Xixona) also lies within easy reach of the provincial capital. This town, just 27km (17 miles) from Alicante on the N-340, is renowned for the manufacture of *turrón*, an exotic sweet of Moorish origin, made from ground almonds, orange-blossom honey, egg white and sugar, and traditionally served by the Span-

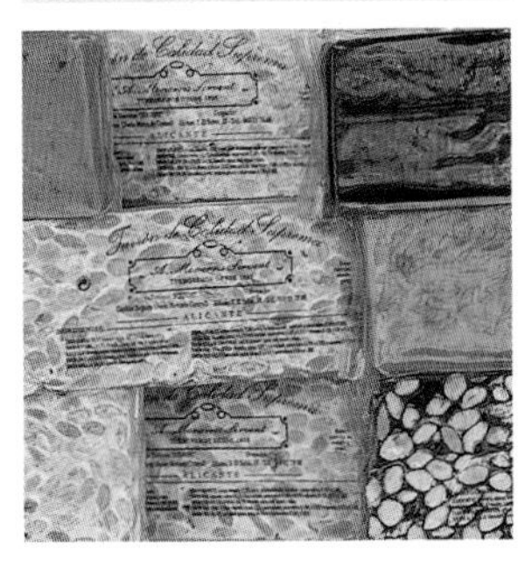

ish at Christmas time. There are several different varieties to choose from *(see box on page 31)*. You can learn all about this popular confection on a tour of El Lobo factory, founded in 1725. There's even a small museum on the premises.

The N340 continues northwards to cross the high Sierra de la Rossa over the Port de la Carrasqueta (1,024m/ 3,360ft). About 8km (5 miles) before you reach Alcoy, a road branches off to the left to the **Parque Natural del Carrascal de la Font Roja**. This stretch of woodland, which has been protected as a nature reserve ever since the 14th century, is named after a fountain, 'the Red Spring', at its heart. Unlike almost all other woodlands in eastern Spain, the woods include many deciduous species of trees, such as oak, ash and maple. In between them are several determined specimens of yew growing at their southernmost limit in Europe.

Parque Natural del Carrascal de la Font Roja

If you feel like some exercise, there is a three-hour walk to the summit of **El Menajador**. On the way, look out for the unusual *pozos de nieve* or *neveras* (ice-pits). It gets very cold up here and farmers used these cellars to store ice to sell in nearby markets.

Alcoy, known for its fiesta

Alcoy

Alcoy (Alcoi) is 56km (35 miles) from Alicante. Don't be disappointed by this grey industrial town, for it manufactures some of Spain's most popular sweets: *peladillas* (Marcona almonds coated with sugar). Sometimes pine kernels are sugar-coated, too, and known as *pinyonets*.

Alcoy is even more famous for its annual 'Moros y Cristianos' Festival: one of the most colourful and exuberant traditional fiestas in the province *(see page 88)*. If you're here out of season, the costumes, worn year after year, will be on display in the 17th-century **Casal de Sant Jordi**.

The **Museo Camilo Visedo** nearby houses a fascinating collection of Iberian clay sculpture taken from a settlement in the Sierra Serreta.

Castle Route

Inland, Alicante province is characterised by its castles, strategically positioned by ever-vigilant Romans, Moors and Christians. The castle of **Castall**, just off the Ibi-Villena road, is one of the most dramatically located in Spain. It was built by the counts of Castalla, but left incomplete.

The castle at Sax

Further along the Villena road is the medieval castle of **Biar**, a well-restored national monument which is surrounded by a double wall. There are magnificent sweeping views of the valley from the castle battlements.

Continue now to the town of **Villena**, which is the furthest point away from Alicante (64km/40 miles) on this tour. Here the **Castillo de Atalaya**, noted for its double walls and a type of high, eight-turreted tower rarely found south of Madrid, also has national monument status. It was built by Moors, though considerable additions were made to the building in the 15th century.

The Tesoro de Villena, priceless Bronze Age gold artefacts discovered in a clay jar in the riverbed, are exhibited at the **Museo Arqueológico** (open Tues–Fri 10am–2pm, Sat 11am–2pm; free), within the 16th-century Palacio Municipal (opposite the tourist office) and attest to the artistry of Villena's early inhabitants.

Swing south from Villena along the N-330 to **Sax**, site of the Roman town of Saxum. The towers of the original Roman castle, which has been fully restored, are still a look-out point. Back on the N-330 you soon come to **Petrel**'s Moorish castle, reputed to have fabulous treasure buried in its grounds. Other medieval fortresses are found along the C-3212 road to **Elda**, and beyond, at **Monóvar**. Elda itself is noted for excellent wine and lace-making. The town was the birthplace of the famous writer, José Martínez Ruiz, better known as Azorín.

From Elda, follow the signs to **Novelda**. Miraculously, in the midst of this industrial town is a perfectly preserved Art Nouveau house, the **Casa Modernista** (Calle Mayor 24; open Sept–July Mon–Fri 9am–2pm and 4–6pm, Sat 11am–2pm; free), furnished in the style of its period, which was saved from demolition in 1975 by a local savings bank. You'll also find yet another Moorish castle set high on a hill. This one is the **Castillo de la Mola**, erected on the site of a Roman fort. It has an unusual triangular tower dating from the 13th century. Right next to it you'll see a strange structure reminiscent of Gaudí's still unfinished Templo de la Sagrada Familia in Barcelona.

If, after all this castle-viewing, you still haven't had enough, a few kilometres further on in **Aspe**, you'll find *las ruinas* (the ruins). Local people will direct you to the castle, which they never call by that name. From here you can head back to Alicante, situated just 28km (17 miles) away.

Castles in Spain

The Costa Blanca has a good share of Spain's 5,000 officially classified castles. Some of them are well preserved, while others have been restored. For 700 years Moors and Christians fought each other for their possession and they frequently changed hands.

Each castle has a specific purpose, history and name. *Alcazabas* are fortresses built by Moors in isolated places. *Castillos guerreros* were built by Christians on sites specially chosen for their strategic positions. And then there are the castle citadels, the *alcazares*. Some of the Moorish *alcazares* are magnificently preserved, enclosing gardens with fountains. Christians replaced the greenery with functional courtyards in their rather severe *alcazares*.

Want to own a castle? The Asociación Española de Amigos de los Castillos (tel: 913 191 829, <www.castillosasociacion.es>) works for the preservation of castles and advises owners on grants available.

NORTHERN COSTA BLANCA

The Costa Blanca's reputation is largely based on the stretch north of Alicante that takes in a great variety of scenery, from lush valleys planted with orange orchards to the forbidding cliffs and crags around Jávea and Calpe. The resorts along this coast are just as varied; while Benidorm is renowned for its high-rise architecture and high energy nightlife, Jávea is conspicuously low-rise and an altogether quieter and calmer place. Calpe and Denia, meanwhile, manage to combine both these aspects of the Costa Blanca.

High-rise heaven

Benidorm's 186-m (610-ft) Gran Hotel Bali is Spain's tallest building. There are 310 buildings over 35m (115ft) in height, giving Benidorm a claim to have the most skyscrapers in the world after New York.

Benidorm

Twin crescent-moon beaches offering some 7km (4 miles) of golden sands, coupled with an outstanding climate, have made **Benidorm** one of Spain's most popular resorts. But it wasn't always so. Despite the efforts more than a hundred years ago of a local entrepreneur, who hoped to bring holiday-makers to the area by a regular stage-coach service, large-scale tourism didn't come to Benidorm until the early 1960s. Since then, masses of apartment blocks and hotels have sprung up and the town has become known as an international party city. Millions of visitors pack into the place over the year.

Love it or hate it, Benidorm is thoroughly cosmopolitan; restaurants here serve bacon and eggs, sauerkraut and smorgåsbord. There are bars, cocktail lounges, ritzy restaurants, modern hotels and a vast choice of discos and nightclubs. The resulting racket contradicts claims that the town's name derives from the *valenciano* words for 'sleep well'; in fact it comes from the Arabic 'Benidarhim' ('sons of Darhim'), which was the name the Moors gave the original settlement here.

The delightful **old village**, the size of a postage stamp, is tucked away on the spur of land that divides the two beaches. A fort stood here until 1812, when British and Spanish troops blew it up while dislodging the French during Spain's War of Independence, leaving only ruins. The greatest concentration of shops and entertainments is to be found around the original village. Away from the beaches there's no end to the amusements, from bowling alleys to water slides.

The most developed of the two beaches is the **Playa de Levante**. You can get a great view of its panoramic skyline from either end: from the **Balcón del Mediterráneo** next to the old town or from the rocks of the **Rincón de Loix** at the foot of the Sierra Helada, a mountain range that stops the further expansion of Benidorm in this direction.

The beach at Benidorm, high-rise capital of Spain

The other beach, **Playa de Poniente**, has developed more slowly than Levante but its popularity and reputation have been assured by the building of Spain's tallest hotel, the **Gran Hotel Bali**, which towers 52 floors and 186m (610ft) above it. It is only expected to remain Benidorm's tallest building until 2010, however, when a 200-m (650-ft) residential block is due for completion.

The two beaches look across a sound to the **Isla de Benidorm**, a wedge-shaped rock of an island and a bird sanctuary which is uninhabited except for a summer bar. It's a good spot for a picnic and a swim, although the water is deep. Glass-bottomed boat trips from Benidorm take 20 minutes each way.

Benidorm was once regarded as a downmarket resort aimed at single holidaymakers but, since the late 1980s, it has been actively encouraging families to visit. Among its attractions for kids are a theme park and two animal parks.

Isla de Benidorm, a short boat trip away

Terra Mítica theme park in the hills outside Benidorm (Camino al Moralet, Carretera Benidorm-Finestrat; open late Mar–mid-June Thurs–Mon 10am–8pm, late June daily 10am–8pm, July–mid-Sept daily 10am–1am, mid-Sept–Oct Sat–Sun 10am–8pm; check <www.terramiticapark.com> for hours; admission fee) has rides, shows and attractions in five themed areas: ancient Egypt, Greece, Rome, Iberia and 'the Islands'.

Mundomar (open daily Mar–Dec from 10am; admission fee; tel: 965 869 101; <www.mundomar.es>) specialises in marine and exotic animals, and claims to have the largest dolphinarium in Europe. Next to it is a waterpark with pools, slides and other attractions.

Terra Natura (Foia del Verdader; open daily from 10am; admission fee; tel: 902 522 333; <www.terranatura.com>) is a fun and educational mix of nature and the civilisations of the earth. In its grounds, cages and compounds there are 1,500 animals from 200 species, 54 of which are endangered.

Villajoyosa

A short way to the south of Benidorm by the main N332 road, past the Casino Costa Blanca *(see page 89)*, is **Villajoyosa** (La Vila Joiosa). Despite being overshadowed by its bigger, brasher neighbour, Villajoyosa is the administrative centre for the Marina Baixa district, the name by which the northern Costa Blanca has always been known by the locals.

The main road goes straight through the town without revealing much, but turn off and wind your way towards the sea through the narrow streets of the old town and suddenly you will see a group of house fronts in striking blues, reds and yellows. It is said that they were traditionally painted such bright colours so that fishermen out at sea could recognise their houses and see what their wives were up to.

Apart from its busy fishing port, La Vila is also home to Roman, Moorish and Visigothic remains, as well as Spain's

The bright coloured façades of Villajoyosa

oldest chocolate factory. The **Museo del Chocolate** (open Mon–Fri 9am–6pm, Sat 10am–1pm; free) offers half-hourly tours explaining the local chocolate-making tradition.

The town comes to life during the last week of July when the Moors and Christians fiesta takes place. Many of the 23,000 inhabitants parade and fight in richly costumed companies – *los piratas, los tuareg* and *los moros del Rif* among them – re-enacting the defeat in 1538 of the Algerian pirate Zala Arráez, a Mediterranean scoundrel who started it all by sacking the castle in a daring dawn raid.

If you dress the part and can stay on your feet for the fiesta's duration, you can join the ranks of *Els Pollosos* ('the Lousy Ones' in the *valenciano* dialect), a 'mercenary' company. You can take part in the famous Moorish attack, still faithfully acted out in imitation of events more than four and a half centuries ago. What with all the cannon-firing and colourful acting, the excitement can reach fever pitch.

Inland from Benidorm

From anywhere on the northern Costa Blanca, inland Spain looks like one brooding mountain range after another. Few visitors bother to leave the coast and explore these heights, although coach parties regularly visit Guadalest.

If you have a car at your disposal there are many scenic routes winding through the mountains that will take you immediately away from the crowds. Although there are few signposted hiking routes, the hills are good walking country *(see box on page 83)*. Stop almost anywhere and you will be on silent slopes fragrant with rosemary, thyme and lavender, and dotted with rock roses and orchids.

Guadalest

The most popular trip inland from the northern Costa Blanca is to **Guadalest**, a village built by the Moors on a dauntingly rocky site more than a thousand years ago. It has lost little of its allure to modernity because access to the old part of the village – effectively one street and one small square – is restricted by a tunnel carved through 15m (50ft) of solid rock. The fortress above the village withstood both an earthquake in 1644 and attempts by the Austrian Archduke Charles to blast his way into possession of Guadalest during the War of the Spanish Succession. Despite the coach tours, Guadalest is still relatively 'unheritaged'. Because of the irregularity of the site and the shortage of space for buildings, the church belfry had to be placed on an adjacent pinnacle of rock where it sits as if posing for a photograph.

Miniature marvels

For such a small place, Guadalest has more museums than you might expect, including two collections of miniature art, with such wonders as a camel passing through the eye of a needle; an ant playing a violin; and an El Greco painting reproduced on a grain of rice.

The church and detached belfry at Guadalest

Touring the Mountains

From Benidorm, drive south on the motorway to Villajoyosa, then take the road that leads to **Sella**. The countryside is fairly undistinguished, until suddenly you look down on the emerald-green waters of the **Amadorio Dam**, a favourite haunt of fishermen and discerning picnickers. Within another 5km (3 miles) you arrive at Sella village, dwarfed beneath an extraordinary plateau.

From Sella, the road winds higher through terraced hillsides filled with vineyards until it reaches its highest point at **Puerto de Tudons** (1,015m/3,330ft). About 8km (5 miles) further on, a secondary road leads to **Penáguila**, an exquisite old Moorish village with a sturdy ruined castle.

Near the town is a little-known garden, the **Jardín de Santos**, which was laid out by an aristocratic family in the 18th century but is now in public ownership.

At **Benasau**, the Sella road meets the CV70. To the west (16km/10 miles) lies Alcoy *(see page 33)*; to the east Confrides, a picturesque mountain town and beyond it Guadalest *(see page 41)*. Beyond Guadalest, follow the road down towards the coast which brings you to **Callosa d'En Sarrià**, surrounded by orchards of medlar trees and a centre for honey production, where you can taste many different flavours before you decide which to buy.

From Callosa you can get back to Benidorm via **Polop** and **La Nucia** or continue the tour by taking the Parcent road. Follow it for 2.5km (1½ miles) and make a right-hand turn at the entrance to the **El Algar** waterfalls, a tumbling oasis beneath the massive Sierra Bernia formed by a tributary of the River Guadalest. Leave your car in the parking area and walk to the 27-m (90-ft) falls.

You can swim beneath the falls in chilly waters, then picnic by the cool leafy pools above. It's easy to get away from crowds in this pleasant spot, but if you're in the mood for company, you'll find lots of people in the restaurants near the car park.

El Algar waterfalls

The next stop is **Tárbena** (10km/6 miles further along the C-3318), a mountain village perched amid cultivated terraces at 567m (1,860ft) and famed for its delicious sausages. They're made from a secret recipe handed down to the present-day villagers by their Mallorcan ancestors, who came here in the early 17th century as part of an official repopulation scheme.

After Tárbena comes the finest scenery of all: bold, terraced mountains, wide undulating valleys and scattered farms connected by mule tracks. In spring the countryside is covered with the pink and white of almond blossoms, but the road is for all seasons, with groves of gnarled olive trees alongside it, their leaves blowing silver in the evening light. Follow the road to **Coll de Rates**, 500m (1,640ft) above the wide orange-grove and vine-filled plains that sweep up to Jávea, Denia, Gandía and the deep-blue Mediterranean. Further on, take the road to **Jalón** (Xaló), where in the late summer farmers sell muscat grapes to passers-by, and you can buy some of the strong local wine. The Jalón valley is also a popular place for eating out in inexpensive country restaurants. Alternatively, carry on past **Orba** to **Benidoleig** and visit the prehistoric caves, **Las Calaveras**. Here high-domed ceilings drip with stalagtites, and human bones more than 50,000 years old have been found.

After a further 6km (3½ miles), you arrive at the coastal motorway from where it's around half an hour's drive back to Benidorm or about an hour's drive north to Valencia.

Altea

Some 10km (6 miles) north of Benidorm is **Altea**, one of the Costa Blanca's most picturesque and tranquil coastal towns. It was an important Phoenician port and the Moors named it Altaya, meaning 'Health for All', but not before they had destroyed the first settlement and rebuilt the town. The 257 steps that climb steeply above the main shopping street, the **Avenida Fermín Sanz Orrio**, lead to the old village. Here the streets are almost always full of people, who congregate in local bars and restaurants. Altea has a number of art galleries and a stunning arts centre just northwest of the old town, where concerts and exhibitions are held regularly.

On Sundays and fiestas, traditional games of *pelota* are played in the narrow streets leading off Altea's church square, where you will find the Virgen de Consuelo church with its distinctive tiled roof, blue with a white geometric design. *Pelota* players strike the ball with their bare hands against walls, doors and windows, which are protected by grilles. A craft market is held outside the church on summer evenings and there's also an arts centre that offers an events-packed programme.

Picturesque Altea

The best of the local beaches, most of which are pebbly, is at **Albir**, between Altea and the Sierra Helada.

Calpe and the unmistakable Peñón de Ifach

Calpe

The town of **Calpe** (Calp), 12km (7½ miles) from Altea, is popular with tourists for its long sandy beaches, notably **Puerto Blanco** and **Playa de la Fossa-Levante**, which have excellent sports facilities. Calpe is famous for the dramatic volcanic rock that separates the beaches. Thrusting out of the sea to a height of more than 335m (1,100ft), the **Peñón de Ifach** is a Rock-of-Gibraltar lookalike and forms the Costa Blanca's most distinctive landmark. As it is home to 400 species of plants and is visited by some 80 species of birds, including peregrine falcons, it is protected as a nature reserve. There is a visitor centre at the base of the rock and a path leading to its summit which affords wonderful views in all directions. You don't have to be a mountaineer to climb it, just reasonably fit. Half-way up is a man-made tunnel which leads to the eastern side of the rock and provides an easier ascent. On the way up, you can admire the wild flowers, and in autumn and winter you may catch sight of Audouin's Gull – a rare species with dark-olive legs and a black-banded red bill. Take a jacket as there can be a breeze blowing as you get near the top. It is also a good idea to carry a bottle of water.

The **town centre** of Calpe is built on a steep slope at some distance from the beaches, the port and Peñón. It has an old Moorish quarter, a few remaining fragments of its medieval walls and a Mudéjar-Gothic church.

If you have time, follow the coastal road from Calpe to **Moraira**, where flats and villas fill terraced hillsides high above rocky coves. Otherwise, take the main Alicante–Valencia road, which passes inland through rich agricultural country to **Gata de Gorgos** – a town noted for cane, basket-work and furniture.

Jávea

Jávea (Xàbia), 27km (17 miles) from Calpe, sprawls between pine-covered Cape Nao to the south and Cape San Antonio to the north. It is ideal for a quiet family holiday, especially in spring when the town is magical with the scents of lemon and orange blossom. Citrus fruit became the region's principal cash crop around the turn of the 20th century when grain and the 17th-century windmills of Cape San Antonio were abandoned.

There are two town centres in Jávea. The older part stands on a low hill a short way inland on the site of an

Jávea: old and new

Jávea has become a magnet for foreigners wanting to set up home in the sunshine, and there are vast estates of modern houses extending into the countryside. But there are still some of the handsome older houses that usually incorporate a *riu-rau*, an arched stone porch where grapes were hung to dry into raisins.

Beach bar in Jávea

Iberian settlement. It surrounds a 16th-century church which was built to serve as a fortified refuge in case of invasion or pirate attack. Many of the houses along the streets of the old town – as well as the town hall and cinema – are made from the characteristic tosca sandstone which is mined locally.

The other part of Jávea lies around the **port** and its modern church, inspired by the ribs of a ship's hull. Also here is the main beach, where development has been kept low-rise in accordance with council planning policy.

But the real charm of Jávea lies in its short but heavily indented coastline extending southwards from the main beach. Pirates and smugglers once found hiding places among the cliffs, caves and inlets around the headland of the **Cap de la Nau**, where there is now a lighthouse and restaurant. **Granadella Cove**, among pinewoods at a discreet distance from the town, is popular with those who want to get away from the crowds and the touristy restaurants.

Denia

To the north, Jávea is protected by the sprawling hump of the **Montgó Massif**, which rises to a 753-m (2,470-ft) high summit and meets the sea defiantly at the rugged headland of Cabo de San Antonio. On the other side of both cape and mountain is Jávea's nearest neighbour, Denia, 10km (6 miles) away. If you want to tackle the peak, this is the side to do it from. Montgó is a nature reserve carpeted with wild flowers in spring and early summer. Climb it for a view of the coast and out to sea as far as the island of Ibiza, 100km (62 miles) away, which is connected to Denia by ferry.

Denia is larger than Jávea and if it has less charm it makes up for it by having a more distinguished pedigree. In the Middle Ages it was briefly the capital of its own small Moorish kingdom and it still shelters under its **Arab Castle** which now contains an **archaeological museum**.

Immediately below the castle is the harbour where, as in most of the Costa Blanca's working fishing ports, you can watch the day's catch being auctioned on the quayside when the boats return in the afternoon. Behind the harbour is the pretty old quarter of **Baix al Mar**, which is a pleasant place for a stroll. Denia has two beaches. The main one is **Les Marines**, looking onto the Gulf of Valencia. **Les Rotes**, meanwhile, is rockier and good for snorkelling and diving – there are several scuba diving schools ready to escort you under the water for the first time.

Just outside Denia, near Vergel, is a well-kept **Safari Park** (open daily 10am–7pm;

Baix al Mar

Produce of the region

admission fee) with animals galore, a fine dolphin show, a children's amusement park, refreshments and restaurants.

Gandia

At **Gandia** (32km/20 miles north of Denia on the N-332), in the province of Valencia, just beyond the official extent of the Costa Blanca, you may be tempted to spend all your time on the 13km (8 miles) of splendid beaches or along the town's broad promenades, where restaurants serve up the local speciality, *fideuá*, a kind of seafood paella in which vermicelli is used instead of rice.

But it's worth taking a closer look at the town that once prospered from the manufacture of silk and had its own university. From its glory days, one building of quiet majesty has survived: the **Palacio Ducal de los Borja** (by guided visit only, hourly, Tues–Sat 10am–2pm and 4.30–8.30pm, Sun 10am–2pm; admission fee). In 1485, Rodrigo Borja (who became Pope Alexander VI but was later implicated in murder and debauchery) was granted the title of Duchy of Gandia. His great-grandson, Francisco (1510–72), fourth Duke of Gandia, abandoned worldly pleasures to join the Jesuit order after the death of his wife and was canonised by Pope Clement X in 1671. The palace, now owned by the Jesuits, is entered via a Gothic courtyard and has superbly decorated apartments within. Particularly worth seeing are the superbly tiled floors depicting the four elements and the duke's private chapel.

Játiva

Játiva (Xàtiva), a 'city of a thousand fountains', huge plane trees and a sprawling fortress, was probably founded by Hannibal in 219BC. Europe's first paper was made here in the 11th century, and both the painter José de Ribera and two infamous popes, Calixtus III and Alexander VI, were born in the town. The popes were members of the Borja family, better known to history as Italy's notorious Borgias.

Seek out Játiva's late-Renaissance **Colegiata** (Collegiate Church) in the Plaza de Calixto III. Just opposite is the 15th–16th century **hospital**. It's noted for a splendid façade designed in the ornate 15th-century Plateresque style. Find time, too, for the well-presented **Museo Municipal de l'Almodi** (open Sept–June Tues–Fri 10am–2pm and 4–6pm, Sat–Sun 10am–2pm; June–Sept Tues–Fri 9.30am–2.30pm, Sat–Sun 10am–2pm) at Carrer de la Corretgeria 46, where

Many splendid historic buildings can be found in Játiva

a portrait of King Felipe V can be seen hanging upside down. In the courtyard round the corner, the 11th-century **Pila de los Moros** (Moorish Basin) was once used for ablutions. The figures decorating the basin are rarely seen in Muslim art, since Islam forbids human and animal representation.

Directly above the old town, the **Ermita de San Feliú** (Saint Felix's Hermitage) commands a wide view. Although it has been a Christian bastion since the third century, it was a pagan sacrificial site long before that. Continue uphill to the fortress (open Tues–Sun 10am–7pm, until 8pm Oct–Mar) which is, in fact, two castles. Ramparts connect the smaller pre-Roman **Castillo Menor** (Minor Castle) with the Roman and post-Roman **Castillo Mayor** (Major Castle), once notorious for its dungeon. Disgraced princes and other noblemen were confined here, their only solace being the ruined 15th-century chapel adjacent.

The castle and Saint Felix's Hermitage

Inland Sights

Albaida, a candle-making town

Leave Játiva on the C-340 and drive up into the highlands, where thick-fleeced sheep and isolated farmhouses complete a memorable vista. Pass through **Albaida**, renowned for its candle-making, and **Onteniente**, an industrial town, to picturesque **Bocairente**. Visit the village during late summer for the festival of folk dancing or in February for the Fiesta of Moors and Christians. The sombre bull-ring was hacked from solid rock.

Bocairente's **Museo Arqueológico** (Archaeology Museum) is noteworthy for its collection of Stone-Age pottery, and the parish church exhibits important paintings by Juan de Juanes, Ribalta and Sorolla. In the hills northeast of the town are the **Covetes de Moros** (Moorish Caves). Some were later lived in by hardy Christian holy men. You can walk to them from the town – follow the signs.

There's a good walk uphill from **Agres**, a short distance to the east of Bocairente, into the **Sierra Mariola**. This mountain range is rich in aromatic herbs which attract an equivalent number of butterflies. Below the summit of **Mont Cabrer** (1,390m/4,448ft) are the ruins of two domed *neveras*. This word has come to mean 'fridge' in Spanish, but before the days of electricity and cooling systems, these ice-pits were built high up on north-facing slopes and packed with snow during the winter months which would turn into ice. Later in the year, this ice would be brought down to the villages on the backs of mules to be used for the preservation of meat and fish.

VALENCIA

Founded by the Romans in 138BC, Valencia later prospered as the capital of a far-flung Moorish kingdom until El Cid briefly recaptured it at the end of the 11th century. In 1238 Jaime I, El Conquistador (whose banner and sword can be seen in the Museo Histórico Municipal), reconquered the city and proclaimed the Kingdom of Valencia.

City Sights

Today, Valencia is Spain's third largest city, boasting a wide range of sports and cultural facilities. Most of its monuments are within walking distance of the **Plaza del Ayuntamiento**, the triangular main square, which is presided over by the town hall. The most central and spectacular of the sights is its **cathedral** (open Mon–Fri 10am–6pm, Sat 10am–5.30pm,

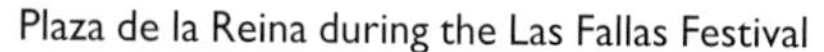

Plaza de la Reina during the Las Fallas Festival

La Lonja, the silk exchange

Sun 2–5.30pm, until 6.30pm daily in summer; admission fee), begun in 1262 on the site of a Moorish mosque. It is a mix of styles, with most parts dating from the 14th and the 15th centuries. Its octagonal Gothic bell tower, known as **El Micalet**, is a symbol of the city and, if you can bear to climb the 207 steps, the view from the top is spectacular. A chapel in the cathedral contains what is said to be the Holy Grail.

Once bounded by the river Turia – its course was diverted to avoid flooding and the dry bed turned into a ribbon of gardens – Valencia has always been fed by the prodigiously fertile area of land that surrounds it (the *huerta*, or 'garden') and for more than a thousand years disputes over irrigation water have been efficiently settled by the *Tribunal de las Aguas* (Water Council). This is a group of eight men who meet every Thursday at midday outside the cathedral's Door of the Apostles. Business is conducted verbally in *valenciano* (the local language), with all decisions being final.

If you want a taste, both metaphorically and literally, of the natural produce that flows into the city from the *huerta*, and from the sea, you should dip into the modernist **Mercado Central** (Central Market; open daily until around 2pm). Built between 1910 and 1926, it is an irregular, eight-sided, iron-girder-and-glass building where you will find an enticing array of fresh meat, fish, vegetables and fruit. Outside the market you can buy the dish to cook paella in, also called a *paella* – they come in a range of sizes and you have to specify how many people you are cooking for. Opposite the market is **La Lonja** (the Silk Exchange; open Tues–Sat 9.15am–2pm and 4.30–8pm, Sun 9.15am–1.30pm; free), which dates from the late 15th century. One of the finest secular Gothic structures in Europe, it is famous for its **Hall of Pillars** where finely crafted helicoidal columns curve graciously up to the roof.

Of Valencia's museums, the **Museo Nacional de Cerámica** (open Tues–Sat 10am–2pm and 4–8pm, Sun 10am–2pm; admission fee), housed in the astonishing Palacio del Marqués de Dos Aguas, is a gem and among its treasures it has hundreds of glorious glazed tiles *(azulejos)* for which the city is famous. The city's major art collection, held at the **Museo de Bellas Artes** (open Tues–Sun 10am–8pm; free), has paintings by Bosch, El Greco, Goya and Velázquez, and a definitive collection of 15th-century Valencian art.

Flamingos at L'Oceanogràfic

The town's **Serrano** and **Quart** medieval gateways, which survived the demolition of the medieval walls in the 19th century, are formidable reminders that such defensive fortifications were vital in centuries past.

Just outside the city centre is the unmissable **Ciudad de las Artes y las Ciencias** (City of Arts and Sciences). The sprawling complex of futuristic-looking buildings and parklands is dedicated to fun and learning. **L'Hemisfèric** (daily screenings), an IMAX cinema and planetarium built in the shape of a gigantic open eye, was designed by Valencian architect Santiago Calatrava. Calatrava also designed the **Palacio de las Artes**, a concert hall with a huge open-air auditorium, and the **Museo de las Ciencias** (Science Museum) which is full of interactive exhibits. **L'Oceanogràfic**, an aquarium with killer whale and dolphin shows, was designed by Felix Candela.

Beautiful beaches

Better beaches can be found if you follow the coast road south from Valencia beyond El Saler. This also takes you past the freshwater lake of Albufera, one of the prime wetland areas of Europe, which is bordered by a maze of paddy fields producing rice for paella and Valencia's other staple rice dishes.

Port and Beaches

The Oceanogràfic is as close to water as many visitors to Valencia get. Although the city looks from the map as if it is by the sea, unlike Alicante, it isn't. Rather, it has its back to the sea with its **port** and **beaches** 3km (2 miles) from the centre. You can take a bus to them down the Avenida del Puerto, but more pleasant ways to get there include metro line number 5 and the swish modern tram from the Pont de Fusta station (across the riverbed from the Torres de Serrano; take metro line 4 in the direction of Doctor Lluch and get off at Les Arenes). A broad promenade follows the sandy beach for 2km (1½ miles) and at the port end is a row of renowned restaurants specialising in paella.

Apart from its monuments and waterfront, Valencia is also much visited for its nightlife. There are bars and clubs aplenty in several parts of the city, but the best place to begin if you don't know the city is in the restored medieval quarter of the **Barrio del Carmen** near the cathedral.

SOUTHERN COSTA BLANCA

Santa Pola

The fishing port and resort of **Santa Pola** (18km/11 miles south of Alicante on the N-332) has an extraordinary number of restaurants. Nearby waters, particularly rich in prawns and red mullet, provide all manner of restaurants, both on the beach and in the town, with some of the best seafood on the coast. If you prefer to see fish and shellfish still living, or just want to know what you are going to be eating, Santa Pola has a delightful municipal **aquarium**, which shuns tropical fish in favour of giving an idea of the life in local waters. The town also has a 14th-century castle and several good beaches with fine white sand. You can catch a ferry from Santa Pola to the island of Tabarca *(see page 30)*.

Thousands of pine, palm, and eucalyptus trees, planted to control shifting sand dunes, shade the beaches at **Guardamar del Segura** (17km/10 miles south again on the N-332), a fishing centre. Spiny lobsters are a speciality of restaurants here.

Torrevieja's Salt Pans

Torrevieja's salt pans are the largest salt-producing lakes in Europe and are of both economic and ecological importance. Sea water is channelled into the lagoons and left to reach a critical density through evaporation. Then the salt is extracted, cleaned, ground up and deposited in conical piles. Most of it is exported for use in the manufacture of foods and chemicals, and for de-icing roads in Scandinavia. The salt pans are protected as a nature reserve because they are home to numerous species of waterfowl including, most spectacularly, flamingos. The pinkish tinge to the water is caused by the high level of salinity and the presence of a particular crustacean.

Torrevieja

The beach at Santa Pola

From here, take the road a further 15km (9 miles), past the salt flats of La Mata, to **Torrevieja** (Torrevela). The long-vanished 'old tower' from which Torrevieja took its name has been replaced by a new one, which suitably symbolises this unashamedly modern town. More than a mere summer resort catering for package holiday-makers – although it is that as well – Torrevieja has turned itself into a centre for 'residential tourism'. A massive programme to encourage the building of low-cost homes in recent decades has encouraged thousands of people from northern Europe to retire, start new lives or live on permanent holiday here in the sunshine. This new demographic trend co-exists with Europe's largest and oldest salt industry *(see page 58)*. To find out more, visit the **Museo del Mar y de la Sal** on Calle Patricio Pérez 10 (open Tues–Sat 10am–1.30pm and 5–9pm, Sun am only). There are few other sights to see here apart from the gorgeously over-the-top 19th-century **casino**, which has been renovated to perfection.

In August Torrevieja pulsates to the music of the Habaneras festival. The theme is the lively song form of the same name (remember Bizet's *Carmen*?), brought back from Cuba during the 19th-century salt-export voyages. The festivities include musical competitions, concerts and shows by leading – sometimes international – companies.

Further down the coast road you will get to a string of growing resorts forming a summer holiday centre – La Zenia, Cap Roig and Dehesa de Campoamor.

The Moorish Legacy Inland

Four historic towns – Elche, Crevillente, Orihuela and Murcia *(see page 71)* – line the N-340 from Alicante. The most distant of them, Murcia, is only about 80km (50 miles) away and all four can be visited in a couple of days. Various cultures have influenced these towns, but the Moorish legacy is predominant.

Elche

Thousands upon thousands of date palms overwhelm the eye in **Elche** (Elx), a city as old as the Iberians and a UNESCO World Heritage Site. Palms were originally planted in this location by the Carthaginians in 300BC. Nowadays they still thrive here, just as the Moors described them, with 'feet in water, heads in the fire of heaven'. Elche's palms are watered by an irrigation system built by the 10th-century Moorish ruler Abderramán III, and surround the town of some 180,000 inhabitants on three sides. Part of this forest has been en-

Royal Palms

Two date palms in the Huerto del Cura supply the Spanish royal household with fruit. The specially chosen trees were dedicated to Spain's reigning monarchs, King Juan Carlos and Queen Sofía, shortly after their accession to the throne. The palms were first watered with wine by the King and Queen. Signs with the names of the monarchs were then hung on the trees by caretakers, who scaled the slippery trunks to cut bunches of dates for the royal couple to sample.

Theirs aren't the only palms with a royal pedigree. The famous *palmera imperial* was dedicated to Empress Elizabeth of Austria during the visit she made to the grove in 1894. Another tree provided Otto of Austria and Hungary with dates. With more than a thousand palms, many of them more than 200 years old, the Huerto del Cura is a noble sight, even by royal standards.

El Huerto del Cura, where trees are dedicated to royal visitors

closed as a private garden called the **Huerto del Cura** (Priest's Grove), which is celebrated for its cactus, pomegranate and orange trees, and, above all, for the *palmera imperial*. This male tree of exceptional age and size has seven branches growing from one main trunk. The *palmera imperial* and many other trees in the grove have been dedicated to visiting royalty and celebrities, such as Claude Debussy and the Nobel Prize-winning scientist Severo Ochoa.

Overlooking the grove's lily pond is an exact replica of the famous bust of *La Dama de Elche* (The Lady of Elche; *see picture on page 13*). The original, from the 4th century BC and now housed in Madrid's Archaeological Museum, remains something of a puzzle more than a hundred years after it came to light. If you look beyond the exotic headdress, you'll see why attributions are difficult to make: the face could be male or female, Spanish, Greek or Eastern. To visit the place where the bust was discovered, go to the nearby hamlet of **La Alcudia** (open summer Mon–Sat 10am–2pm and 4–8pm, Sun 10am–2pm, winter Mon–Sat 10am–5pm, Sun 10am–3pm; admission fee). Exhibits of Iberian and Roman finds are displayed in the excellent museum.

On the way, you'll see palms that look like giant asparagus tips. *Encapuchadores* bind these male trees in spring to produce the pale bleached fronds that are used in Palm Sunday celebrations. These branches, once suitably blessed, are said to conduct lightning, and you'll see them attached to houses all over Spain. The female palms make a less esoteric annual contribution of 10,000 tons of dates, which ripen in December and are highly prized for their juicy sweetness.

Iglesia de Santa María

Back in Elche, there are more palm trees to see and more luxuriant tropical foliage to admire. You can dine and dance in the frond-slatted shade of the **Parque Municipal**, which also features citrus trees and a noisy frog pond.

Not far from the Municipal Park, the **Calahorra Tower**, 'Guardian of Elche', once formed part of the main gate in the long-vanished wall that surrounded Elche in Moorish times.

Next to the tower you'll see the blue dome of the **Iglesia de Santa María**. The church was constructed in the 17th century and rebuilt after being damaged during the Civil War. Every August a spectacular form of sacred theatre, *El Misterio de Elche* (The Mystery of Elche), is performed here by an amateur cast of priests, civic dignitaries and other local people. The play has been presented in Elche for more than five centuries. The music, Gregorian and traditional, is sung in old *lemosín*, which is a variant of Occitan. During the rest of the year you can see a multimedia presentation of the play at the **Museo Municipal de la Fiesta**.

Across the main road from the church you can't miss the solid **Palacio de Altamira**, with its square towers. This Moorish palace formed part of the city wall. The Vinalopó River, spanned by a bridge here, supplies the water that is still carried to the *huertas* via canals that were originally dug by the Moors.

A short distance from the palace going towards the city centre, you will come upon the **Ayuntamiento** (Town Hall), with its fine Renaissance façade and Gothic door. Stand back for a good look at the clock on the neighbouring 14th-century **Torre del Concejo**, a former watchtower. The carved mechanical figures of Miguel Calendura and Vicente Calendureta appear to ring the hours and quarter hours respectively, as they have done since 1759.

Crevillente

Nineteenth-century travellers sped through neighbouring Crevillente in fear of the notorious bandit James the Bearded. Today, Crevillente's industrial appearance similarly induces haste. But those unattractive factories produce 70 percent of Spain's handsome woven rugs and carpets, and many welcome visitors.

Crevillente was the birthplace of the Arab surgeon Al-Xafra, and during his 13th-century heyday the town was an excellent place in which to fall ill. The progressive Moor's treatise on 'wounds, inflammations and tumours' may sound hair-raising today, but his treatment of broken bones by means of padded splints, traction and bitumen casts was actually centuries ahead of its time.

The **Museo Municipal Mariano Benlliure**, (closed for restoration), next to the church, has a collection of bronze, marble and clay works by the modern sculptor Mariano Benlliure (1868–1947), among them likenesses of the famous men of his day. It also houses some of his *pasos* – floats containing life-size or larger sculptures of holy figures which are a feature of religious processions, particularly during Holy Week.

The peaceful cloisters of the Colegio de Santo Domingo

Orihuela

Situated on the usually peaceful banks of the River Segura, **Orihuela** is a few kilometres off the busy A-7. Water is drawn from the Segura for the irrigation of the town's groves and fields. When the expulsion of the *moriscos* (converted Moors) – once the town's agricultural labourers – threatened the fertility of Orihuela's crops in 1609, townspeople hid away enough *moriscos* to ensure a good harvest.

The **old university**, on the northern outskirts of the city, was constructed in the 16th and 17th centuries. It's now a school, the **Colegio de Santo Domingo** (open

Tues–Sat 9.30am–1.30pm and 4–7pm, until 8pm in summer, Sun 10am–2pm; free). The baroque cloisters, magnificent staircase and beautifully tiled refectory are lovely. Near the school you'll see all that's left of the town's original wall, the **Puerta de la Olma** (Elm Tree Gate).

Tiled seat, Orihuela

Now make for the Plaza de Caturla, a small square on the outskirts of Orihuela. From here you can climb a hill to the old **Seminario de San Miguel** which offers panoramic views of Orihuela below and a ruined castle above.

There are many historic buildings to see in Orihuela; the town remains much as it was centuries ago, despite an earthquake in 1829 and present-day industrialisation. The Gothic **cathedral**, begun in the early 14th century, with spiral rib vaulting and ornamental grille-work, is considered one of the region's finest. The **Museo Diocesano de Arte Sacro** (Diocesan Museum of Sacred Art; open Mon–Fri 10am–1.30pm and 4–7pm, Sat 10am–1.30pm; admission fee) features a famous painting by Velázquez, called the *Temptation of Saint Thomas Aquinas*. The fine Romanesque **cloister** was moved here from a nearby convent that suffered damage in the Civil War. It was erected around an early Gothic cross that is Orihuela's austere monument to Spain's war dead.

Orihuela's **Museo de Semana Santa** (Easter Week Museum; open Mon–Fri 10am–1pm and 4–6pm, until 7.30pm in summer, Sat 10am–1pm; admission fee) features a bizarre curiosity, the *Paso de la Diablesa* (She-Devil Statue), which has been scaring sinners since 1688 when Nicolas de Busi carved it.

COSTA CÁLIDA

The Costa Cálida, the coast of Murcia province, extends from just south of Torrevieja to the border with Andalucía and is among the last stretches of Spain's Mediterranean shoreline to be developed for tourism. Leaving aside the ribbon-shaped resort of La Manga del Mar Menor and the naval base of Cartagena, it is still relatively easy to find a quiet space somewhere along this coast.

The Mar Menor

The focal point of the Costa Cálida is the **Mar Menor**, the 'Lesser Sea', which is a sheltered saltwater lagoon separated from the Mediterranean by a 22-km (14-mile) sand bar. It is often described as 'a natural swimming pool' because its waters are calmer than those of the Mediterranean. They can also be several degrees warmer.

The main resort here is **La Manga del Mar Menor**, which forms a ribbon of high-rise development all the way along the sand bar. Seen from the landward side of the lagoon it

Glorious Mud

The Mar Menor is not only a pleasant place to splash about in because it is warm and salty, but it is supposedly good for you as well. The water is rich in mineral salts said to relieve the symptoms of arthritis and rheumatism. At Lo Pagán, at the northern end of the lagoon, you're likely to see bathers wallowing in the mud which has been found by researchers at the University of Murcia to be full of positive and negative ions, calcium, magnesium, potassium, fluoride, chlorides and sulphates. Spas in Los Alcazares, San Pedro de Pinatar, Santiago de la Ribera and especially Lo Pagán will be happy to relieve you of your money in return for a formal mud bath and treatment.

forms a surreal skyline: a jagged line of apartment blocks and hotels that seem to be standing on the water. But at least La Manga makes no pretensions to be anything other than a modern resort where the beaches and marinas face both ways: onto the Mediterranean and the Mar Menor.

The sea at La Manga

Far more attractive are the small old-fashioned resorts on the inland side of the Mar Menor: **Los Alcazares**, which has 7km (4 miles) of sandy beaches, **Santiago de la Ribera** and **Lo Pagán**. These places grew as a result of the mineral-rich water in the lagoon *(see box opposite)*. From Santiago, you can take a boat trip to the largest of the six islands in the Mar Menor, the **Isla Mayor**. This is also called the Baron's Isle because an aristocrat fleeing from the Russian Revolution is said to have found a home in exile here.

The Mar Menor is a sporting paradise. Anywhere around the lagoon you can sign up for courses in sailing, water-skiing and windsurfing, taking avantage of its tranquil waters. Above the lagoon's southern shore there is a *de facto* private sports centre (open to non-residents) at **La Manga Club** which has three championship golf courses, innumerable tennis courts of all surfaces (the Davis Cup has been held here) and both indoor and outdoor swimming pools. The Club also has training facilities for football and cricket.

The fastest way from the Mar Menor to Cartagena is via the motorway but there is a slower way around the coast through a harsh but interesting landscape of industrial archaeology. Long before tourism this part of Murcia's coast was a centre for mining. In Roman times thousands of slaves toiled here to extract lead and silver, and forests were cut down to make pit props and to keep fires for smelting constantly burning. Centuries of mining have left their mark. The road between Portman and La Unión winds through hills scarred by mining, with old shafts and ruined pit-head buildings scattered here and there.

Cartagena

The compact, bustling city of **Cartagena** (26km/16 miles south of Los Alcazares on the N-332) is the legislative capital of Murcia province. It was a major naval port long before St James is said to have landed here with the Gospel in AD36. The Carthaginians named it Quart Hadas, Punic for 'new city', when they arrived in 230BC from Carthage in North Africa. In 218, their leader, Hannibal, enriched by the local silver mines, mustered his vast army of elephants here to march against the Romans, who retaliated by conquering Spain and renaming the city Carthago Nova, New Carthage. Romans, Visigoths and Moors all squabbled over this strategically positioned town, which was sacked by Sir Francis Drake in 1588 and taken by Archduke Charles of Austria in 1707 during the War of the Spanish Succession.

Head for the port and the large waterfront **Plaza del Ayuntamiento**. The big, grey, cigar-shaped object

Local authors

Cartagena is the birthplace of Spain's leading medieval theologian, Isadore of Seville (c. 560AD), and the contemporary thriller writer, Arturo Pérez Reverte (1951).

Cartegena's strategic position made it a focus of attention

you'll see on view here is a submarine, which was built by the local inventor Isaac Peral and launched in 1888, 10 years too late to make a world record. Just north of the Plaza, stop for a coffee at one of the open-air cafés on the traffic-free Calle Mayor. Then head uphill to the **Castillo de la Concepción** at the highest point of the city. The castle dates back to Roman and perhaps even Carthaginian times. It's surrounded by the **Parque de las Torres**, a beautifully landscaped vantage point. The pepper-pot lighthouse in the park, of Roman or Moorish origin, wrecked many a marauding ship when it was blacked out by the defenders of Cartagena.

One glance over the almost land-locked harbour explains why Andrea Doria, the 16th-century Genoese admiral, remarked that the Mediterranean had only three safe ports: June, July and Cartagena. You'll also see why Cartagena is called the 'City of Castles'. Almost every hill has one: to the north-

Art Nouveau façade in Plaza San Francisco

east there's a Moorish fort; no fewer than four ruined fortresses guard the harbour entrance; and two more, still in good repair – the **Atalaya** and **Galeras** castles – protect the sea-front arsenal, which is of vital importance to Spain's military.

Immediately west of the Castillo de la Concepción are the ruins of the 13th-century **Iglesia de Santa María la Vieja**. Its Romanesque portal is a 19th-century restoration, but the Roman and Byzantine columns and Roman mosaic floor are authentic. In the adjacent Calle del Cañón, look out for the **well-head** with weathered rope-marks that are supposed to have inspired St Isidore, the youngest of a 6th-century Visigoth duke's four saintly children, to argue the merits of perseverance. On the waterfront adjacent to the city centre, the **Museo Nacional de Arqueología Marítima** (National Underwater Archaeological Museum; open Tues–Sun 10am– 3pm; free) on Muelle de Alfonso XII has exhibits of shipwreck booty and a replica of a Roman gallery housing a collection of Roman and Greek jars.

Quite a long trek to the northwest is the **Museo Arqueológico** (Archaeological Museum; open Tues–Fri 10am–2pm, Sat–Sun 11am–2pm and 5–8pm; free), noted for its exceptional collection of Roman mining tools.

The Southern Costa Cálida

The Costa Cálida southwest of Cartagena has escaped the worst ravages of mass tourism and there are only two resorts along it of any size. Beyond Cabo Tiñoso is **Puerto de Mazarrón**, which lies 34km (21 miles) west of Cartagena. The last city on Murcia's coast is **Aguilas**, about 50km (30 miles) further southwest. It was laid out in a grid pattern during the Enlightenment under the auspices of King Charles III and his ministers for the export of agricultural products. Later, large quantities of silver, lead and iron were shipped from the town. Today Aguilas is predominantly a town given over to tourism. As well as sandy beaches there are 35 coves in the vicinity, many untouched by tourism. The waters around the Isla del Fraile and the cliffs of Cabo Cope are popular with divers.

The town itself is chiefly of interest for its 16th-century castles, and the town hall is a handsome neo-Mudéjar building. Near it are gardens with a swan fountain known locally as 'the turkey on the pond'. In the Paseo de Parra a small steam engine stands on a plinth as a monument to the British South Eastern Railway Company and its contribution to the economic development of the town.

MURCIA

Like Elche and Orihuela, the provincial capital of **Murcia** has been a rich oasis since the time of the Moors. Its market gardens, second only to Valencia's, are watered by the River Segura and yet another Moorish irrigation system. Today's provincial capital was a favourite city

A young woman from Murcia

of the Moors and in 1224 they even made it the capital of a small *taifa*, or break-away kingdom. The most celebrated local hero was the powerful yet benign Cardinal Belluga y Moncada. This warlike prelate thwarted the all-conquering Archduke Charles of Austria in 1707, during the War of the Spanish Succession, preventing Charles from advancing by flooding Murcia's fields, then attacking the invader with a small army which he had recruited at his own expense.

Murcia's cathedral stands in the plaza named in honour of Cardinal Belluga. Construction of the **Catedral de Murcia** (on the site of a mosque) began in 1394. There's not a hint of the 14th century in its splendid western façade, however. This baroque renovation, one of Jaime Bort's celebrated designs, was undertaken when the original Gothic front suffered irreparable damage in a disastrous flood of the Segura in 1735. You can climb the round tower that rises from the north side of the building for an impressive view.

Inside the cathedral, the **Capilla de los Vélez** (Chapel of the Vélez) is remarkable for its Plateresque decoration. This highly ornamental style is typical of 16th-century Spain. The *coro* (choir) shelters a *Christ* by Francisco Salzillo, one of many supremely realistic works by this native son of Murcia. Others (a *Saint Jerome* and a *Virgin*) are on display among the chalices and *retablos* of the Museo Diocesano, adjoining the cathedral.

Catedral de Murcia

Before you leave the sanctuary, visit the **Capilla Mayor** (Main Chapel). The strangest of the cathedral's treasures is contained in an urn here: it is the heart of

Puento Viejo over the River Segura

Alfonso el Sabio ('the Wise'), which was bequeathed to Murcia by the 13th-century king long before his death.

Go out of the cathedral on the north side and walk across Plaza Hernández Amores to the cool and classy **Calle de la Trapería** (Street of Secondhand Merchants). But don't look for bargains here; the name of this pedestrian thoroughfare belies the elegance of its shops. At the north end you come upon the **casino** (a private club, not a gambling establishment), with spirited turn-of-the century decor. The entrance hall, an exact copy of the Hall of Ambassadors in Seville's Alcázar, and the ladies' lavatory – with its ceiling of cherubs – are the most magnificent rooms. During the casino's heyday, the pedestrian **Calle de la Platería** (Street of Silversmiths), at right angles to the Trapería, was full of practising craftsmen. Flower stalls in the Plaza de las Flores are open every morning.

Northwest of the city centre is the **Ermita de Jesús church** and its impressive **Museo Salzillo** (open Tues–Sat 10am–2pm and 5–8pm, Sun 11am–2pm; admission fee). The highly important group of sculptures gathered here represents every facet of Francisco Salzillo's work. During a career that spanned the 18th century, Salzillo produced large processional figures still carried in Holy Week celebrations, and small intimate carvings, some of them on a miniature scale.

Also worth a visit is the **Museo de Arqueología** (open Mon–Fri 10am–2pm and 4–8pm, Sat 10am–1.30pm; admission fee), on the Avenida Alfonso, which traces the history of the region from Roman times.

Waterwheels have been operating in the Murcia region for more than a thousand years. You can see one at **La Ñora**, 6km (3½ miles) from Murcia city centre. The original wheel has been replaced with a steel one, but the Moorish system is otherwise unchanged. A few kilometres further on, at **Alcantarilla** in the direction of Granada on the N-340, the **Museo de la Huerta** (Agriculture Museum; open summer Tues–Fri 10am–8pm, Sat–Sun 10.30am–1.30pm and 4–6pm, winter Tues–Fri 10.30am–6.30pm, Sat–Sun 10.30am–1pm and 3–6pm; admission fee) adjoins a second steel waterwheel. The museum's exhibits present all the aspects of Murcian country life, including traditional furnishings.

Salzillo sculpture

Inland Murcia Province

Apart from Murcia city, Cartagena and the Mar Menor, the province of Murcia receives relatively few visitors but there are many places worth beating a path to even if the intervening countryside is often dry and even a little drab. Water from the local rivers has been insufficient to sustain either agriculture or property development, so some is now being diverted to the region from the Tajo.

Wine and Spa Towns

The Río Segura creates an irrigated green corridor of its own with the spa of **Archena** as its main town. The thermal sulphur and salt baths here once attracted rheumatic Romans *(see box below)*. There is another spa, **Fortuna**, in the hills to the northeast. Keep going and you will reach the wine towns of **Yecla** and **Jumilla** which have long languished in the shadow of more famous centres of Spanish wine production but are gradually making a reputation for themselves.

Following the course of the Segura, you come to **Calasparra**, a centre for rice growing, with a protected certificate of origin. The especially fine paella grain is available everywhere in town.

Taking the Waters

For a change from the refreshing sea, you can unwind the way the Romans did, sweating it out in a spa. The area has two important and accessible spas, Archena and Fortuna. They date back to the times of the Moors and the Romans.

Choose either simple public baths where a few euros buy a place for the day or expensive private facilities in a hotel such as the one at Archena. This isolated spa occupies a spectacular site in an oasis of towering trees; the waters clearly work for them.

Caravaca de la Cruz

A most rewarding excursion into the interior is to **Caravaca de la Cruz**. This town was once a possession of the Knights Templar and later of the Knights of Santiago. Its castle was founded by the Moors, but what you see today is mostly a baroque construction erected in the 17th century to commemorate a miracle that occurred four centuries before. It said that on 3 May 1232 when the Moorish overlord of Caravaca asked a captive Christian priest to say mass, the priest refused because he did not have a cross on his altar and on cue two angels flew into the castle carrying a double-armed cross. Overawed by the spectacle, the Moorish chief asked if he could be baptised.

Cehegín, next door to Caravaca, is notable for its medieval quarter, and 14km (9 miles) to the north is the pretty hill village of **Moratalla**, a popular hiking centre.

Lorca

It's easy to speed past **Lorca**, in the far south of the province, on the motorway into Andalucía, but it's well worth a look around. For centuries it was a frontier town between the Moors and the Christians, as witnessed by its castle which originally had 35 towers. It prospered most in peacetime during the 17th and 18th centuries when so many fine buildings were erected that a British traveller likened it to

A castle towers over Caravaca de la Cruz

Oxford. Notable baroque buildings in the main square include the **town hall**, a former prison built between 1677 and 1739, which comprises two halves connected by an arch spanning the street. Across the square is the **Colegiata de San Patricio**, the only church in Spain that is dedicated to St Patrick. Calle Alamo runs left past the town hall to the splendid Casa de los Guevara. The eponymous family proclaimed their prosperity with a fantastic baroque portal.

Lorca stages a lavish Easter parade on Good Friday, when thousands of people put on a show of Biblical splendour dressed as Nebuchadnezzar, Solomon, Cleopatra, the Tribes of Israel and the Queen of Sheba.

WHAT TO DO

Much of your Costa Blanca holiday will be spent on the beaches – and there are hundreds of them to choose from. Some slope gently and are thronged with people; others are tucked away in coves beneath spectacular cliffs, assuring all the privacy and tranquillity of a desert island.

There are Red Cross offices on the most popular beaches. Flags are used to advise swimmers of sea conditions: a green flag means the sea is safe for swimming, while a red flag warns of danger. Normal precautions apply here as elsewhere: beware especially of water-skiers and jet-skiers.

Most of the beaches with fine sand are situated to the north of Alicante. In general, these have been developed as resorts and offer all sorts of facilities – everything from speedboats and parasails to windersurfers and kiteboards to deck chairs and sunshades. The further south you go, the fewer provisions you'll find for water-related activities. The beaches towards the south can be pebbly, while the sand is usually coarse. But the area beyond Cartagena remains relatively uncrowded.

Away from the beach, there's swimming at the aquaparks in Alicante, Benidorm and Torrevieja.

OUTDOOR PURSUITS

Boating

Most beaches offer boats for hire, but the resorts with a variety of craft to choose from are generally on the Mar Menor. Benidorm is usually the most expensive resort. Pedal boats or small sailing dinghies can be hired on many beaches.

Festive dress, Lorca

Nearly all coastal resorts have a Club Náutico (yacht club), but the Mar Menor, with shallow and wind-assured waters, is the place for the keen sailor.

Snorkelling and Scuba Diving

Snorkelling is at its best off cliffs and near rocks. Offshore, snorkellers are required, for safety reasons, to tow a marker buoy. For more profound sea experiences, try scuba diving. Several centres provide equipment, a dive boat, expert local knowledge and sometimes tuition as well. A diving permit is required under Spanish law. Unless you speak reasonable Spanish and know where to go, it's best to let your chosen diving centre deal with the documentation. Diving is generally safe: the ripples, currents, tides and giant predators found in other seas scarcely exist here.

All cliffs and islands, including Benidorm's small reef, offer interesting scuba diving. Local experts will show you where to find air-locked caves, probe modern wrecks that are full of surprises or watch a fresh-water spring bubble mistily from the seabed. The waters around Calpe's Peñón are home to a tremendous variety of sea creatures, including the big-mouthed grouper, the rare zebra-striped bream and the Turkish wrasse.

Windsurfing at Denia

Water-Skiing

Water-skiing is a comparatively expensive sport, so shop around among rival schools for length of runs, number of attempts allowed for 'getting up' and discounts for multiple runs. Serious lessons are usually confined to the early morning when the sea is calmest. For something less energetic, try parasailing; the views are superb.

Cable Ski Benidorm (Playa de Levante, tel: 639 612 713, <www.cableskibenidorm.com>) offers lessons for all abilities, including cable-skiing in which the skier is pulled along by an overhead cable. Denia's Maremoto Jets (Pol. San Carlos 1-b, tel: 966 422 765, <www.maremotojets.com>) specialises in jet skis and rents out motorboats with or without a skipper. Jetski Costablanca.com (tel: 966 850 814, <www.jetskicostablanca.com>) rents out water motorbikes to explore the Sierra Helada area.

Underwater world

Every resort of any size has at least one diving school which will give you an introductory lesson with full scuba equipment. But if you just want to take a plunge with face mask and snorkel, the best places are on the northern Costa Blanca from Calpe to Denia. Try the rocks and coves of the coastline around Jávea.

Windsurfing and Kitesurfing

There are several kitesurfing and windsurfing outfits that hire out equipment for both sports, as well as offer vital tuition. Les Deveses beach (also known as 'La Chimenea') at Denia is considered one of the best places to windsurf on the Costa Blanca. Windsurfing Center Denia (open May–Sept, tel: 649 29 79 59, <www.windcenterdenia.com>) hires out windsurfing equipment, catamarans and kayaks. Club Windsurfing Santa Pola (open July–Sept, Avenida Blasco Ibáñez 55, tel: 965 416 258; <www.windsurfsantapola.com>) hires out boards at Santa Pola's Gran Playa beach.

Walking on a coastal trail

Bird-Watching

Ornithologists should bring their binoculars. The Costa Blanca is crossed by principal migration routes and holds considerable, often unsuspected, bird life. In summer, if you sit by any reasonably quiet river mouth, you may see black tern.

In autumn and winter bird-watchers search cliffs, particularly Calpe's Peñón, for the rare Audouin's Gull: look out for a small, sleek 'herring gull' with dark-olive legs and a heavyish red bill banded in black.

In winter the salt pans at Santa Pola and Torrevieja attract thousands of migratory flamingos, a few of which sometimes stay to breed. *(See also box on page 8)*.

Bullfighting

Despite an increasing number of Spaniards who are anti-bullfighting, the *corrida* tradition continues, especially during fiestas. There are major bullrings in Alicante, Cartagena and

Murcia. Top matadors – qualified *toreros* who fight fully grown half-ton bulls – occasionally appear in Benidorm, while novice fighters can be seen in other tourist centres.

If you want to visit a bullfight, the best seats to buy are *sol y sombra, tendido bajo*, lower stands which are in the sun part of the time and in the shade the other. The first two rows are the most expensive. Admission prices are lower in Alicante than in Benidorm. Tickets everywhere are 20 percent more than the official price when purchased from agencies and as much as 40 percent more from hotels. Whether you have booked in advance or not, try to arrive at the *plaza de toros* with an hour to spare, enough time to watch the crowd and feel the tension rising. The *corrida* always starts on time – even if the clock occasionally has to be stopped.

Fishing

The rivers of the Costa Blanca region may reveal carp and barbel, but don't expect much excitement. The best freshwater fishing hereabouts is at the Amadorio Dam, 4km (2½ miles) from Villajoyosa *(see page 39)*, and, to a lesser extent,

Walking

If you fancy a break from the beach and from sightseeing, the hills of the northern Costa Blanca provide good walking country. But it pays to take a few sensible precautions. Never walk alone, and always tell someone where you are going and how long you expect to be away. Carry water, suncream and a 1:50,000 map. Wear sturdy shoes and, although shorts may seem to suit the climate, long trousers. These will protect your shins from the spiky Mediterranean vegetation that can be uncomfortable to walk through. Although you are more than likely to get a warm sunny day, it can get chilly if you reach a fairly high altitude and you'll be glad that you put a pullover in your bag.

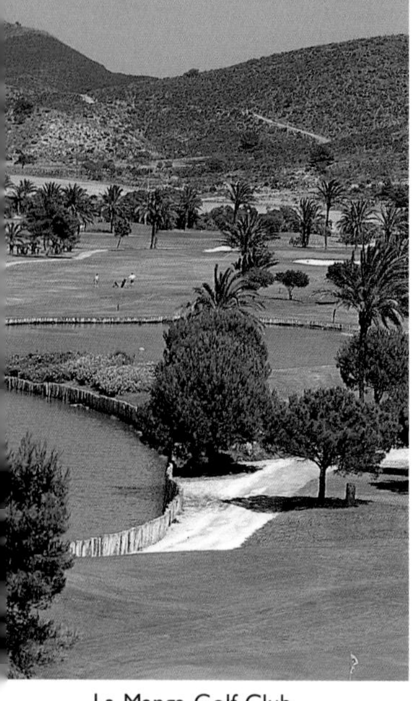
La Manga Golf Club

Guadalest's dam. They hold barbel, the biggest carp, smallish black bass and rainbow trout – introduced in 1977 and still protected. To catch them you'll need a licence with a trout supplement. The season for non-mountain trout runs from the first Sunday in March to 15 August.

There is no national licensing system for fishing; for information ask at a local fishing-tackle shop or tourist information office, or contact the Federación Española de Pesca y Casting at Calle Navas de Tolosa 3, 28013 Madrid, tel: 915 328 352, <www.fepyc.es>.

If you go sea fishing, you will need local knowledge to hook big grey mullet, sea bream, bass and maybe even grouper below quiet cliffs, and mackerel a few kilometres out. In summer you may catch tasty dorada; in late summer, autumn and winter, various species of tuna and swordfish.

Golf

The golf courses on the Costa Blanca are open to visitors but you should still book in advance. Clubs, caddies and, occasionally, electric trolleys can be hired. The two 18-hole Kentucky blue-grass courses near La Manga are the region's lushest, with shady palms. There are also two fine 18-hole courses at Torrevieja's Club Villamartín, as well as two good nine-hole courses: Altea-la-Vieja's Don Cayo, where the hills test legs as well as golfing skills, and the San Jaime Club de Ifach between Calpe and Moraira.

Horse Riding

There are ranches that cater for the tourist trade and provide a quiet seaside jog. Other centres offer good horses, skilled instruction and interesting cross-country riding. Inexperienced riders can enjoy a moonlight excursion, with a barbecue at the end of an easy ride.

For the experienced and saddle-fit there are mountain treks of up to five days, for instance via Altea's Río Algar, or from La Sella, near La Jara. These treks go through orange, almond and olive groves, across rivers and up through pine forests and open moors to real sierra country.

SHOPPING

You will often find the Costa Blanca's best buys off the main streets or in the markets. For the greatest variety and lowest overall prices, shop in the side streets of Alicante. For special items go inland to the place of manufacture, keeping in mind the prices asked on the coast and at home: Guadalest for ponchos and shawls; Gata for cane, basket work and guitars; Crevillente for woven rugs and carpets; Jijona for *turrón*; Ibi for toys.

In general, look out for good prices at hypermarkets outside the major towns.

Regional pottery

Prices everywhere will be on display and you will only be able to bargain at street markets. Beware of *rebajas* (sales); they may be genuine, but reductions are generally few and far between, especially in season.

The Spanish government levies a value-added tax (called IVA) on most items. Tourists from overseas can get a refund on the IVA they have paid on purchases over a stipulated amount. Major tourist shops have forms and details. The refund can be repaid to your credit card.

Shopping hours are generally from 9am to 1pm and from 4 to 8pm. In summer some shops may stay open later. The big Alicante and Valencia department stores stay open during the traditional siesta, which is the quietest time to shop. In the tourist season small shops often stay open on a Saturday evening and Sunday morning. Bakeries and newsagents open in the morning only on most fiestas – but don't count on it.

Paella pan shop in Valencia

Best Buys

A specialist fan makers'

Antiques can be good buys, but beware of fakes. Look for copper and brass, hand-painted tiles and simple oil lamps. If you can find one, and carry it home, you could buy a traditional cradle. Few are authentically antique, but they are decorative and excellent for holding all sorts of things – even babies.

Cuban cigars are exceptional value for money (but US residents are not allowed to take them home). Canary Island cigars are usually cheaper.

Leather goods are no longer a bargain in Spain, though good-quality products may still cost less than at home.

Lladró porcelain has long been a collector's item. The Lladró brothers opened their factory in Tabernes Blanques, near Valencia, in 1958. Opposite is a seconds shop. Less detailed models are sold under the name Nao.

Mat and basket-work has been a local craft for 1,500 years and is not very expensive.

Ponchos and knitted shawls from Guadalest are colourful and attractive.

Rugs woven in Crevillente are hard-wearing and can be made to your own design.

Other souvenirs include pottery, some featuring Moorish designs; bullfight and flamenco posters with your name topping the bill; low-crowned, broad-brimmed Cordoban leather hats; hand-painted fans; elegant *mantillas* (the traditional lace shawls for special occasions); *botas* (soft leather wine bottles; avoid those with plastic linings); and *turrón*, the sweet made in Alicante and Jijona *(see page 31)*.

ENTERTAINMENT

The Costa Blanca and particularly the Costa Cálida offer a range of entertainment from high-brow art to informal beachside cabaret. Alicante and Benidorm offer the most choice followed by Elche, Torrevieja and Murcia.

The region's main **theatre** is the Teatro Principal in Alicante (Plaza de Ruperto Chapi, tel: 965 203 100, <www.teatroprincipalalicante.com>), which stages concerts, ballet and musicals as well as dramatic productions. Another top venue for dance and all types of music is the Auditorio de Murcia (Avenida Primero de Mayo, tel: 968 341 060, <www.auditoriomurcia.org>)

For lavish spectacle you can't beat Benidorm Palace (Avenida Severo Ochoa, Benidorm, tel: 965 851 660 <www.benidorm-palace.com>), which puts on a show of music and dance and lays on dinner too.

There are **cinemas** in all the major towns. Most show films dubbed exclusively into Spanish, but there are occasionally screenings of foreign films in their original language – marked 'VO', *versión original* – on advertisements. Try

Moors and Christians in Alcoy

For most of the year Alcoy is a calm and business-like town but for three days a year it goes to war during its annual fiesta of Moors and Christians. The best day to attend is 22 April, if you can stand the crowds. In the morning the Christian army enters the town marching 10 abreast with much pomp and ceremony. In the afternoon it is the turn of the Moors in their extravagant oriental costumes. The fiesta ends on 24 April with a ritualised confrontation between the two sides, in which the Moors temporarily capture a castle before St George appears to award victory to the Christian forces.

seeing a film in a *cine de verano* (summer-only open-air cinema), where you watch the stars on screen under the real stars. There's one in Alicante and two in Benidorm.

If you have money to burn, there are four **casinos**: two branches of Casino Mediterráneo at Villajoyosa and Torrevieja (<www.casinomediterraneo.es>), the Gran Casino Murcia (<www.orenesgrupo.com>) and the casino that forms part of La Manga Club on the Mar Menor *(see page 67)*.

The Moors and Christians Festival at Alcoy

Fiestas

Even the smallest village in Spain holds at least one fiesta a year in honour of its patron saint or the Virgin Mary, and it will also mark national religious holidays, including Easter, Assumption and Corpus Christi, with some event or other. Larger towns manage to fit in several celebrations a year. The result is a busy calendar of traditional festivities on the Costa Blanca with something going on somewhere almost all of the time.

Forget about peace and quiet or sightseeing when there is a fiesta in progress as everything shuts down and streets are often blocked to traffic to allow a procession to go past. Just enjoy the atmosphere of everyone of all ages being in the streets and mixing together, with pretty much any behaviour being tolerated as long as it doesn't harm anyone

Las Fallas in Valencia

else. You are almost certain to be offered the typical food and drink of the region and get the opportunity to dance to live music. Almost every fiesta is built around a carefully organised programme, including processions, folk dances, marching bands and usually some spectacular fireworks.

The characteristic fiestas of the region are the parades and mock battles of Moors and Christians, best seen in Alcoy *(see page 88)* and Villajoyosa *(see page 40)*, and the bonfires of Las Fallas in Valencia and those of Las Hogueras, which are at their height in the city of Alicante. Murcia, meanwhile, excels at Easter Week processions.

Folk Dancing

The best-known traditional dances on the Costa Blanca are the *jota valenciana* and *jota murciana*. Sets of vivacious performers either dance alone facing a partner or in pairs. Their steps can either be vigorous or stately and gracious.

The dancers are accompanied by musicians playing the guitar or instruments introduced into the region by the Moors – the *dulzaina* (flute) and *tamboril* (tambourine). The rhythms go all the way back to the Iberians and reflect a diversity of influences, from Moorish to Aragonese and Castilian to Cuban.

Nightlife

The mild climate and seaside location make the large resorts favoured places for residents and visitors to spend a night on the town. It can even be fun just to hang out in the streets people-watching as the temperature cools down, but there are plenty of dedicated nightspots to enjoy if you want to find some action. Don't go out too early or you'll think the action has finished already: at 11pm people are still digesting their dinner and probably won't go out for another hour. A really good night begins late and ends late: it often finishes with breakfast well after the sun has come up. (You can still fit in a few hours' sleep before heading for the beach). The key to staying the course is to pace yourself: don't drink too much, and make sure you eat something every so often.

In Alicante the best area to look for *bares de copa* (nocturnal drinks-only bars as opposed to day-time tapas bars), cafés and *cervecerías* (bars serving a range of different beers) is the old city centre, universally known as the El Barrio. Several of them serve up live music: ask around or ask in the tourist information office to find out what's on. Later in the night the clubs *(discotecas)* open and do not close until well past dawn.

There are plenty more bars and clubs between the Avenida Alfonso X El Sabio and the Explanada de España. In the summer many people head for the Playa de San Juan or even Benidorm for more action. The beach areas are also the best places to head for if you have a family in tow. In Spain parents commonly take their children out with them

A Valencian bar

everywhere. Naturally, they avoid the dark, noisy bars and sweaty clubs in favour of cafés and restaurants where there is space for kids to run around outdoors. *Heladerías* (ice-cream parlours), *horchaterías* *(see page 102)* and fast-food outlets all stay open late in the holiday season.

CHILDREN'S ACTIVITIES

Kids are welcomed everywhere at any time in Spain, and most parents take them with them when they go out. For a babysitter, ask at your hotel reception desk, or, if you are on a package holiday, ask your rep. Places for a family day out include:

- **Terra Mítica** theme park near Benidorm *(see page 39)*.
- **Safari parks** at Vergel, near Elche, and in the Sierra Aitana, near Penáguila.
- **Aquaparks** (open summer only) at Alicante, Benidorm, and Torrevieja.
- **Mundomar** in Benidorm *(see page 39)*, which claims to be the largest dolphinarium in Europe.
- **Oceanogràfic** in Valencia, a gigantic aquarium (part of the City of Arts and Sciences – *see pages 56–7*).

Dolphins at L'Oceanogràfic

Other attractions and activities for children include the **Ibi Toy Museum**, and the **Museo de Miniaturas** (Museum of Miniature Art) at Guadalest where you can see Leonardo da Vinci's *Last Supper* painted on a grain of rice. Or take a trip on the **Limón Expres**, an old-fashioned narrow gauge train that runs from Benidorm to Gata de Gorgos.

Calendar of Events

January. Everywhere (6 Jan): Epiphany – the arrival of the Three Kings.
March. Valencia and nearby towns (week to 19 Mar): *Las Fallas* – gigantic sculptures are set up in streets and squares and burnt at midnight.
March or April. General, especially Cartagena, Murcia and Lorca: *Semana Santa* (Holy Week) – major nationwide week-long Easter celebrations; deeply religious and often lavishly costumed. Murcia: *Fiesta de la Primavera* (Spring Festival) – folklore and fantasy, parades, fireworks and fanfares begin the week following Holy Week.
April. Alcoy (22–24 Apr): *Moros y Cristianos* (Moors and Christians) – brilliantly costumed parade and sham battle on or around St George's Day.
June. Alicante and neighbouring towns (week including the 24th): *Hogueras de San Juan* (St John's Bonfires) – similar to Las Fallas in Valencia, with fireworks and effigies set alight in the streets, plus parades and bullfights.
July. Coastal resorts such as Torrevieja and Santa Pola (16 July): *Virgen del Carmen* – said to bring luck for the year's fishing; an effigy of the virgin is taken out to sea for a blessing, surrounded by fishing boats, followed by fireworks on the beach. Villajoyosa (24–31 July): *Moros y Cristianos* – local historical pageant. Denia: week-long fiesta – includes *Toros en el Mar* (Bulls in the Sea) where the young people of the town chase a bull around a bullring set up on the harbourside until the chaser or the bull, or both, fall into the water.
August. Torrevieja: *Festival de Habaneras* *(see page 59)*. Elche (13–15 Aug): *Misterio de Elche* (Elche mystery play) – public dress rehearsal and performance. Buñol (inland from Valencia): *La Tomatina* (end of Aug).
November. Everywhere (1 Nov): All Saints' Day – the dead are remembered and cemeteries are filled with flowers. Benidorm: *Virgen del Sufragio* – week-long celebrations of the patron saint with various events.
December. Torrevieja (8 Dec): the town's main fiesta – with processions and fireworks. Ibi (28 Dec): the Spanish version of All Fools' Day – men with flour-caked faces *(Els Enfarinats)* choose a mock mayor for the day. Everywhere (31 Dec): New Year's Eve – families and friends gather and eat 12 grapes in time to the chimes of midnight.

EATING OUT

Far more interesting than the so-called 'international' cuisine, the hearty local dishes are worth seeking out: ingredients come fresh from the sea or the farm and are served with a wide choice of the region's excellent vegetables. The majority of tourist hotels and restaurants specialise in caution, with menus causing neither rapture nor recrimination. Many restaurants close on Sunday evenings and for a month or two in summer or autumn, so it's wise to check before going.

Restaurants

The Spanish eat late, but in tourist areas you will be served lunch from 1pm and dinner from 8 or 9pm. Bills tend to include tax and service charge, but it is usual to leave a small tip: more than 5 percent is generous.

A bargain *menú del día* (menu of the day) is often on offer. There are restaurants which specialise in them, offering three good courses, bread and a jug of very reasonable *vino de la casa* (house wine).

If you are saving up for a special meal, or just economising, fill up on traditional *potajes*, thick soups full of vegetables, in unpretentious restaurants with one fork or none. Spain's golden potato omelette *(tortilla española)* makes another excellent budget meal.

Bars and Cafés

Bars and cafés are at the centre of the country's social life: where workers take an early morning drink and businessmen negotiate; where old men play cards and friends meet to watch the world go by from shaded pavement tables. Bar prices always include service, but a small 5 percent tip is

Dishing up paella

usual. You will pay up to 15 percent more for service at a table, especially outside, and even more in tourist centres.

Soups and Stews

The favourite dish of many visitors is the Andalusian 'liquid salad', *gazpacho*. This chilled, tasty soup, based on chopped tomatoes, peppers, cucumbers and garlic, is very refreshing on a hot summer's day. Note that *gazpachos* or *gazpacho manchego* is a completely different dish *(see page 98)*.

Michirones is a splendid mixture of broad beans, chunks of ham, paprika, sausage and hot peppers, plus tasty bits of this and that. *Pebereta talladeta* started life as a stew composed of potatoes, pepper and tuna-fish gills, but today thick tuna steaks are often the main ingredient. *Guisado de pavo*, turkey stew, is a gastronomic must: to do justice to this speciality of Orihuela be sure to order it at least six hours in advance.

Oranges in Valencia

Rice and Paella

High-quality rice *(arroz)* has been grown on the Costa Blanca's doorstep since Moorish times; hence the many rice dishes and, king of them all, paella. Spain's most famous dish is named after the large, shallow iron pan in which it is cooked and served. The essence of paella is rice cooked in stock and coloured yellow with saffron – or, more commonly these days, food colouring. The authentic variety is *paella valenciana*, which is made with chicken, rabbit, snails and two types of locally grown bean. There is also a fish and seafood variety, *paella marinera* or *de mariscos*. Beware of inferior dishes calling themselves paella in which any and every ingredient seems to be thrown.

Spaniards only eat paella at midday. A good paella is always made to order, usually for a minimum of two people, and takes about 30 minutes to prepare.

Fish and Seafood

The seafood and fish of the Mediterranean provide some of the coast's most memorable meals. A great favourite is *zarzuela de mariscos*, a variation of a Catalán dish, which combines many different ingredients, just like the Spanish operetta from which it takes its name. Shellfish is served with rice in an unlikely but very tasty sauce of olive oil, ground almonds, assorted spices and chocolate, though local cooks sometimes cheat a bit by adding octopus and other shell-less titbits.

Then there is *langosta* – spiny lobster – as succulent and as expensive as ever, and sometimes priced per 100 grams (be sure to read the menu's small print). *Gambas* are prawns, and *langostinos*, the jumbo-sized version. Try them *a la plancha* (grilled), *a la romana* (fried in batter) or *al pil pil* (in a hot, spicy sauce). *Emperador* (swordfish) is especially good grilled, and *lenguado* (sole) is delicious in batter, grilled, or sautéed in butter. For something different, try *dorada a la sal*: a whole fish packed in wet salt, then baked. It comes to the table in a shiny white jacket that is broken when the fish is cut and served.

Vegetarians

Vegetarian food is fairly uncommon in Spain, although virtually all restaurants will have *tortilla* (potato omelette) and salad on the menu. Other possibilities include *champiñones* (mushrooms, which are generally fried with garlic), *pisto* (similar to ratatouille) and *espárragos* (asparagus).

Oranges

The Arabs are said to have introduced the orange (*naranja* is an Arabic word) to the Costa Blanca because here they found the perfect growing conditions for it: light, warmth and abundant water for irrigation. In spring the blossom of the trees – *el azahar* – emits a sweet and delicate perfume powerful enough to waft into city streets and through car windows. The ripe fruit is picked in winter and fresh oranges begin to appear in shops and on roadside stalls in December. When buying oranges, don't be put off by appearances: a thin scuffed skin and a few leaves still attached are usually signs of sweet, juicy fruit within.

Feeling bullish?

Criadillas are considered a delicacy: more than one tourist-conscious menu has billed them as 'mountain oysters', but they are in fact bulls' testicles.

Meat Dishes

Although rice and fish dishes make up a substantial part of the local diet, meat is also on the menu in the region, although in nothing like the same range and imaginative presentation. Among local meat specialities is *gazpachos* (with a final 's' to distinguish it from the chilled soup). This lusty, well-spiced Costa Blanca dish consists of pork, chicken, rabbit and snails – and perhaps even partridge or pigeon. It's stewed in a large frying pan.

When it's time to splash out, try *cabrito asado* (roast kid) or *cochinillo* (roast suckling pig). Both are expensive delicacies but delicious. *Alioli*, a garlic-flavoured mayonnaise, accompanies many dishes. It's an excellent piquant speciality of the Costa Blanca region.

Dessert and Fruit

Ice cream, fruit, rice pudding and *flan* (crème caramel) are the most popular desserts. In the summer and early autumn you will be spoiled with an enormous array of fruit. The weekly markets – the best place to buy – are full of strawberries, *nísperos* (loquat, a cousin of the lychee), grapes, figs, melons, peaches, apricots, raspberries, pomegranates, grapefruit, lemons, oranges, tangerines, apples, pears, bananas, pineapples and dates.

Tapas

A *tapa* is a mouthful of anything that tastes good, and the variety is enormous: smoked mountain ham, spicy sausages, cheese, olives (some as big as pigeon's eggs), sardines, mushrooms, mussels, squid, octopus, meatballs, fried fish, plus sauces and exotic-looking specialities of the house. The name comes from the practice, sadly almost vanished, of providing a free bite with every drink. The titbit was put on a small plate traditionally used to cover the glass and came to be called a *tapa*, which means lid.

Touring tapas bars is great fun, especially in a town's old quarter. It can be expensive – certainly more than the cost of an orthodox meal – but do try to devote at least an evening to it. The code is simple: one helping is called a *porción*; a large serving is a *ración*; half as much is known as a *media-ración.*

Breakfast

Most Spaniards start the day with *tostada* (toast), a simple roll or the traditional *churro*, a kind of elongated fritter made by pouring a batter-like mixture into a cauldron of hot olive oil. The golden-brown result is traditionally served with hot chocolate for dunking.

Churro being fried

In deference to foreign habits, full breakfast *(desayuno completo)* is served at most tourist hotels. This usually consists of fruit juice, coffee, rolls, eggs and perhaps bacon as well. As oranges grow all around you, freshly squeezed juice is easy to find. Ask for *zumo natural de naranja* (freshly pressed orange juice).

Mermelada means any form of jam. Marmalade lovers should ask for *mermelada de naranja.* If you prefer bitter orange, be sure to specify *naranja amarga.*

Wines and Spirits

Although wines from the north are considered to be Spain's best, the Costa Blanca's and Murcia's *vino* is very drinkable and very reasonably priced. Look for Monóvar, Pinosa and the lighter, less plentiful Ricote (all available in red, rosé or white). Beware of the innocent-looking red Jumilla: its

Spectacular view at the Cap de Nau bar and restaurant

18 percent alcohol content can sneak up on you. The same peril exists with the strong Alicante dessert wine, 10 drops of which were long reckoned to be one of nature's surest cures. Be sure to taste the Costa Blanca's renowned Moscatel wine. It's perfect with dessert and preserves all the sweet, distinctive flavour of the Muscat grape.

Sangría

Iced *sangría* is a perfect hot-weather drink. It is a combination of red wine, brandy and mineral water, plus fruit juice, sliced oranges, other fruit and sugar. Beware: *sangría* can pack a punch, especially when laced with rough brandy, but you can dilute it with soda water and plenty of ice.

A *bodega* is a large wine cellar found in towns and most villages. Wine matured in the enormous, dark barrels that line the walls of the older *bodegas* is not much more expensive than *vino corriente* (ordinary wine) from a modern million-litre vat. Sample before buying, especially the cheaper wines. They cost less than some mineral waters and will be blended to your taste; containers are extra.

Sherry *(jerez)*, a wine fortified with brandy, has been made in Spain for hundreds of years. By the early 18th century, Spain was already exporting it to France.

You will find all the world-famous names on the Costa Blanca, and all at reasonable prices. Pale *fino* is dry and light, while amber *fino*, known as *amontillado*, has an earthier taste. *Olorosos* (which include the brown and cream varieties) are sweet, heavy and dark, and go well with dessert.

Somewhere between the two are the *amorosos*. These are medium dry, light amber in colour, and can be ordered for an aperitif or as a dessert wine. Most sherries can be bought from the barrel, and blended to your own taste.

Cava, the Spanish champagne, is mass-produced and reasonably priced. For a dry variety, look for the description

City bar, Valencia

brut. *Seco* (dry) never really is, and *dulce* is very sweet. Other sparkling wines, *vinos espumosos*, go down well on a hot day if served chilled.

Spanish brandy is a bit heavy and sweet, and bears little resemblance to the best French cognacs. More expensive varieties are smoother.

Liqueurs abound. Many famous foreign brands (especially French) are made under licence and sell at prices below those in their home countries. A glance along the shelves of any bar shows the vast range of Spanish liqueurs. They are mostly sweet and often herbal. Try Alicante's *Cantueso*, made since 1867 and still unknown outside the province.

Other Drinks

Coffee is very good. *Café con leche* is half coffee, half milk; *café cortado* is strong and served with a dash of milk; *café solo* is strong and black. Instant coffee is always available. Coffee without caffeine is called *descafeinado*.

A refreshing summer drink popular all over Spain is *horchata*, which looks like milk but is made from a vegetable root. Always served cold, you can ask for it as a liquid *(liquida)* or semi-frozen *(granizada)*. Drink it straight or copy the locals and dunk soft sweet cake sticks *(fartons)* or crunchy breadsticks *(rosquilletas)* into it.

To Help You Order…

Could we have a table?	**¿Nos puede dar una mesa?**
Do you have a set menu?	**¿Tiene un menú del día?**
I'd like a/an/some…	**Quisiera…**

beer	**una cerveza**	milk	**leche**
bread	**pan**	mineral water	**agua mineral**
coffee	**un café**	napkin	**una servilleta**
cutlery	**los cubiertos**	potatoes	**patatas**
dessert	**un postre**	rice	**arroz**
fish	**pescado**	salad	**una ensalada**
fruit	**fruta**	sandwich	**un bocadillo**
glass	**un vaso**	sugar	**azúcar**
ice-cream	**un helado**	tea	**un té**
meat	**carne**	vegetables	**verduras**
menu	**la carta**	wine	**vino**

… and Read the Menu

aceitunas	olives	**langosta**	spiny lobster
albóndigas	meat balls	**langostino**	large prawn
almejas	baby clams	**mariscos**	shellfish
bacalao	cod	**mejillones**	mussels
callos	tripe	**merluza**	hake
cangrejo	crab	**ostras**	oysters
cerdo	pork	**pimiento**	green pepper
chorizo	spicy sausage	**pollo**	chicken
chuletas	lamb chops	**pulpitos**	baby octopus
cocido	stew	**queso**	cheese
cordero	lamb	**salchichón**	salami
gambas	prawns	**ternera**	veal
jamón	ham	**tortilla**	omelette
judías	beans	**trucha**	trout

HANDY TRAVEL TIPS

An A–Z Summary of Practical Information

A

ACCOMMODATION *(hoteles; alojamiento;*

see also CAMPING and the list of RECOMMEND HOTELS on page 127)

Spanish hotels *(hoteles)* are graded from one to five stars according to the facilities they provide. *Hostales* (one to three stars) and *pensiones* (one to two stars) tend to be less well equipped and correspondingly cheaper.

Most hotels on the coast are impersonal modern blocks; inland, however, there are now many small family-run hotels in picturesque villages or set in their own grounds. If you prefer self-catering you'll find many flats for rent in the coastal resorts, but if you want somewhere with charm, rent a village house or *casa rural.*

I'd like a single/double room.	**Quisiera una habitación sencilla/doble.**
with bath/shower	**con baño/ducha**
What's the rate per night?	**¿Cuál es el precio por noche?**

AIRPORTS *(aeropuerto)*

Alicante's airport, **El Altet**, handles domestic and international flights and is located 12km (7½miles) to the southeast of the city. Taxis are available, or use the airport bus service (6.30am–11pm). Buses depart every 40 minutes.

Murcia-San Javier Airport is located on the shore of the Mar Menor. There is a bus service from the airport to Murcia bus station (daily 5.45, 7.15 and 10.45pm; 45 minutes).

Where's the bus for…?	**¿De dónde sale el autobús para…?**
What time does the bus leave for…?	**¿A qué hora sale el autobús para…?**

Valencia Airport at Manises is 8km (5 miles) from the city. Taxis are available, Metro lines 3 and 5 take you right into the city centre, or there's a direct bus service every 20 minutes (6am–10pm).

B

BUDGETING FOR YOUR TRIP

To give you an idea of what to expect, here are some average prices in euros. However, they must be regarded as approximate, as prices vary from place to place, and inflation creeps relentlessly higher. Prices quoted may be subject to a VAT (IVA) tax of 4, 7 or 16 percent.

Airport transfer. Bus from El Altet to Alicante €1, taxi to Alicante about €15, taxi to Benidorm €50 (more at night).

Camping (per day): adult €3.50–5, child €2.50–4, car €3.50–5, tent €3.50–6, caravan (trailer) or mobile home €5–7.

Car hire (international company). Weekly rate with unlimited mileage, including tax and insurance: economy model €150–200; compact model €230–300. (A cheaper rate may apply if you pay for the hire car in advance.)

Entertainment. Bullfight €30, cinema from €5, flamenco nightclub (including drink) from €20, disco from €10 (sometimes free for women).

Hotels (double room with bath). 5 stars €250, 4 stars €150, 3 stars €75–100, 2 stars €60, 1 star €50.

Meals and drinks. Continental breakfast from €4, *plato del día* €8–10, meal in good establishment from €30–60, small beer €2 (in a nightclub/disco from €5), coffee €1.50, Spanish brandy €2, soft drinks €1.

Sports. Golf (per day) green fee from €50; tennis court fee from €6 per hour, instruction from €10 per hour; windsurfing from €12 per hour; horse riding from €12 per hour.

Taxi. Meters start at around €3. Prices for long distance journeys are usually fixed, so check before starting your journey.

C

CAMPING (*camping*)

There are official campsites along the whole coast. Facilities vary, but most have electricity and running water. Some have shops, small playgrounds for children, restaurants, swimming pools and launderettes. For a complete list of campsites ask any tourist information office or see <www.guiacampingfecc.com> or <www.fedcamping.com>.

May we camp here?	**¿Podemos acampar aquí?**
We have a tent/caravan (trailer).	**Tenemos una tienda de camping/una caravana.**

CAR HIRE (*coches de alquiler;* see also DRIVING)

To hire a car you must be over 21 and have had your driving licence for at least six months – citizens of the EU can use their normal licences; other nationals need an international one.

There are branches of international, national and local car hire companies at Alicante airport and in the main towns and resorts. You can hire a car through a local travel agent, but it is usually cheaper to book and pay in advance rather than to hire a car on the spot. A value-added tax (IVA) of 16 percent is added to the total charge, but will have been included if you have paid before arrival. Fully comprehensive insurance is required and should be included in the price; confirm that this is the case. Most companies require you to pay by credit card, or use your card as a deposit/guarantee.

I'd like to hire a car.	**Quisiera alquilar un coche.**
for one day/a week	**por un día/una semana**
Please include full insurance coverage.	**Haga el favor de incluir el seguro a todo riesgo.**

If you are travelling with children, you can save money and avoid inconvenience by taking your own child or infant car seat with you from home.

CLIMATE

Obviously, summer is the high season on Spain's sunny coasts; this is often the only time the whole family can get away. But if you are able to plan your trip just before or after the school holidays, you'll find prices are lower and accommodation is easier to find. The following chart indicates monthly average temperatures in Alicante.

	J	F	M	A	M	J	J	A	S	O	N	D
max °C	16	17	20	22	26	29	32	32	30	25	21	17
min °C	7	6	8	10	13	15	19	20	18	15	10	7
max °F	61	63	68	72	78	84	90	90	86	77	70	63
min °F	45	43	47	50	56	61	66	68	65	59	50	45

CLOTHING *(ropa)*

Whatever you wear for hot summers will be fine for the Costa Blanca. Have a light sweater handy for the evenings. Between November and March it can be cold, sometimes with winds, so always carry a jacket or something warm. Even in August it's wise to take jumpers when going on excursions to the mountains. When visiting churches, women no longer *have* to cover their heads, but decent dress is expected.

COMPLAINTS

Try to settle the matter with the establishment first. If you can't, ask for an official complaint forms *(Hoja Oficial de Reclamación)*. The original of this triplicate document should be sent to the regional office of the Ministry of Tourism, one copy remains with the establishment complained against and you keep the third sheet.

The consumer's information office (the *Oficina Municipal de Información al Consumidor*) should normally be able to give advice.

CONSULATES *(consulado)*

If you get into serious trouble, seek out the British Consulate, which helps citizens of all English-speaking countries (Australia, Ireland, New Zealand, South Africa and the US).

British Consulate, Plaza de Calvo Sotelo 1–2, Alicante, tel: 965 216 190, fax: 965 140 528, <www.ukinspain.com>.

CRIME AND THEFT (see also LOST PROPERTY)

Spain's crime rate is comparable with the rest of Europe. Hang on to handbags and wallets, especially in busy places such as at a bullfight, open-air market or fiesta. Don't take valuables to the beach. Lock cars and *never* leave anything on view that may tempt a thief to break in and see what else there is. If you suffer a theft or break-in, report it to the local police; you will need to have done so for your insurance claim.

CUSTOMS AND ENTRY FORMALITIES *(aduana)*

Most visitors, including citizens of all EU countries, the US, Canada, Australia and New Zealand, require only a valid passport – not a visa or a health certificate – to enter Spain. Visitors from South Africa must have a visa. If you expect to remain for longer than 90 days, a Spanish consulate or tourist office can advise you of the steps to take.

Although there is no restriction on what items you may bring in with you as a tourist, there will be hardly anything you cannot buy locally, and perhaps, more cheaply. Visitors can bring an unlimited amount of euros or foreign currency into the country. On departure you must declare any amount beyond the equivalent of €6,000.

Check with the customs authority of your own country for duty-free allowances of alcohol, tobacco and other goods.

D

DRIVING

Arrival. If you want to bring your own car to Spain, you will need the car's registration papers, a nationality plate or sticker, a red warning triangle, a Green Card extension to your regular insurance policy, and a bail bond which can be arranged through your insurance company. Your own driver's licence is valid in Spain, but you may want to obtain an international driving permit for extra assurance.

Road conditions. Main roads are adequate to very good and improving all the time. Secondary roads can be bumpy. The main danger of driving in Spain comes from impatience, especially on busy roads. A lot of accidents in Spain occur when overtaking, so take it easy. Spanish truck and lorry drivers will often wave you on (by hand signal or by flashing their right directional signal) if it's clear ahead.

Rules and regulations. Driving is on the right and overtaking (passing) is on the left. Give way to vehicles coming from the right (unless your road is marked as having priority). The use of front and rear seat belts is compulsory.

(international) driving licence	**carné de conducir (internacional)**
car registration papers	**permiso de circulación**
green card	**carta verde**
Full tank, please.	**Llénelo, por favor.**
lead-free/diesel	**sin plomo/diesel**
Check the oil/tyres/battery.	**Por favor, controle el aceite/ los neumáticos/la batería.**
I've had a breakdown.	**Mi coche se ha estropeado.**
There's been an accident.	**Ha habido un accidente.**

You should display a nationality sticker on your car. Always carry your driving licence and/or international driving permit with you. As the police can demand to see your passport at any time, it is also a good idea to carry a photocopy of its important pages (if not the actual passport itself).

Spanish law requires that your car should carry a set of spare headlamp and rear-lamp bulbs, and that you wear a reflective yellow safety jacket (to be kept in the front of the car) before you step out of the car in the event of a roadside emergency. Seat belts are compulsory, and children under the age of 10 must travel in the rear. Motorcyclists and pillion riders must wear crash helmets, and motorcycle lights must always be switched on.

Speed limits in Spain are 120km/h (75mph) on motorways; 100km/h (62mph) on broad main roads (two lanes each way); 90km/h (56mph) on other main roads; 50km/h (31mph), or as marked, in densely populated areas.

Traffic police. Armed Guardia Civíl patrol the roads on motorcycles. In towns the municipal police handle traffic control. If you are fined for a traffic offence, you will have to pay on the spot. The blood alcohol limit is 0.5g/l and there are hefty fines for those caught drink-driving.

Breakdowns. Spanish garages are efficient and spare parts are readily available for most common makes of car. If you are an affiliated member of the RAC, you may call on the services of the Real Automóvil Club de España, tel: 90 40 45 45 (roadside assistance).

Parking. Most towns have blue zones with tickets sold at ticket meters for periods up to two hours.

Distances. The following are approximate road distances between some provincial and regional centres:

Alicante to:	km	miles
Albacete	165	99
Barcelona	520	312
Benidorm	45	27
Elche	25	39
Gibraltar	665	399
Málaga	520	312
Murcia	80	48
Valencia	180	108

Benidorm to:	km	miles
Altea	10	6
Cabo de San Antonio	55	27
Cabo La Nao	65	39
Calpe	20	12
Denia	60	36
Jávea	50	31
Moraira	35	22
Villajoyosa	10	6

Road signs: most signs are the standard pictographs used throughout Europe. However, you may encounter these written signs:

¡Stop/Alto!	Stop!
Aparcamiento	Parking
Autopista (de peaje)	(Toll) motorway (expressway)
Ceda el paso	Give way (yield)
Cruce peligroso	Dangerous crossroads
Cuidado	Caution
Despacio	Slow
Desviación	Diversion (detour)
Peligro	Danger
Prohibido adelantar	No overtaking (passing)
Prohibido aparcar	No parking
Puesto de socorro	First-aid post

E

ELECTRICITY *(corriente eléctrica)*

The standard is 220-volt, though if you are in an old building you may find 125-volt current. If in doubt, check before plugging in your appliances. Sockets take round two-pin plugs, so you will probably need an international adapter plug. Visitors from North America will need a transformer unless they have dual-voltage travel appliances.

What's the voltage?	**¿Cuál es el voltaje?**
an adapter/a battery	**un adaptador/una pila**

EMERGENCIES *(urgencias)*

If you're not staying at a hotel, ring or visit the Municipal Police or the Guardia Civíl. If at all possible, take a Spanish speaker with you, although some police stations in the main tourist areas now have interpreters on staff.

National/municipal police	**091/092**
Guardia Civíl	**062**
Fire brigade *(bomberos)*	**080**
National emergency number	**112**

careful	**cuidado**	fire	**fuego**
help	**socorro**	police	**policía**
stop	**deténgase**	Stop thief!	**¡Al ladrón!**

G

GETTING THERE

By air (see also AIRPORTS). The Costa Blanca is served by Alicante, Valencia and Murcia airports, which are linked by regular flights from the UK and other European cities. The main gateway to Spain from outside Europe is Madrid's Barajas airport. Among the airlines with services from the UK to the region are British Airways <www.britishairways.com>, easyJet <www.easyjet.com>,

Flybe <www.flybe.com>, jet2.com <www.jet2.com> and RyanAir <www.ryanair.com>. There are also charter flights from the UK and Ireland to the Costa Blanca, available generally as part of package tours. It is possible to find your own accommodation and submit this to your travel agent who can then arrange a 'package' with charter flight.

By road. The main access roads from France to the Costa Blanca run to the east of the Pyrenees via Barcelona. Choose between the toll motorway (expressway) or the slower, more congested main road. You can also cross the Spanish border at Puigcerdá near Andorra and from there travel on the N-152 to Barcelona, or go via Pau (France) through the Somport tunnel to Huesca, Zaragoza and continue via Teruel to Valencia. There is a long-distance car-ferry service from Plymouth to Santander in northern Spain (a 24-hour trip) and from Portsmouth to Bilbao; from these two ports you can get to the Costa Blanca via either Zaragoza or Madrid.

By rail. The *Tren Hotel* links Paris with Barcelona. The journey takes about 12 hours. For most other connections you'll have to change trains at Portbou.

A global Inter-Rail pass allows one month's unlimited second-class travel in 30 European countries, including Spain, for residents of the participating countries (for details check <www.interrail.com>). Inter-Rail also issues a pass for travel in Spain which is valid for 3–8 days within one month.

People living outside Europe can purchase a Eurailpass <www.eurail.com> for unlimited rail travel in 18 European countries including Spain. This pass must be obtained before leaving home.

The Spanish National Railways, or RENFE (*Red Nacional de los Ferrocarriles Españoles*, tel: 902 243 402, <www.renfe.es>) also offers unlimited rail travel passes. Another useful organisation for European rail travel is Rail Europe (<www.raileurope.com>).

GUIDES AND TOURS *(guía)*

There is no official agency for guides. Guides are usually attached to local travel agencies and normally accompany their excursions. Freelancers exist, but agree on a price in advance.

We'd like an English-speaking guide.	**Queremos un guía que hable inglés.**

H

HEALTH AND MEDICAL CARE

By far the best solution, to be completely at ease, is to take out a health insurance or travel insurance policy to cover the risk of illness and accident while on holiday. Health care in the resort areas and in the major cities is good but expensive, hence the need for adequate insurance. Residents of the European Union should carry with them the European Health Insurance Card or EHIC (available in the UK from post offices or online <www.ehic.org.uk>), which entitles them to basic free medical treatment within the EU.

Many tourists from northern climes often suffer painful sunburn through overdoing it on the first day or two. Falling asleep on the beach is a common cause. Take the sun in short doses for at least the first few days, and go easy on the alcohol as well. Drink plenty of bottled water *(agua mineral)* to avoid dehydration.

For minor ailments, visit the local first-aid post *(casa de socorro* or *dispensario)*. Away from your hotel, don't hesitate to ask the police or a tourist information office for help.

I need a doctor/dentist.	**Necesito un médico/dentista.**
I've a pain here.	**Me duele aquí.**
a fever/sunburn	**fiebre/quemadura del sol**

Pharmacies *(farmacias)* are usually open during normal shopping hours. After hours, at least one pharmacy per town remains open all night, the *farmacia de guardia.* Its location is posted in the window of all other *farmacias.*

HITCH-HIKING *(auto-stop)*

In Spain, hitch-hiking is strictly forbidden on motorways and toll roads, and not recommended elsewhere.

L

LANGUAGE

Learning a few words of Spanish goes a long way. *Castellano* (Castilian), Spain's official language, is understood everywhere. *Valenciano*, a Catalan dialect, is widely spoken. English, French and German are often spoken in the tourist centres.

Politeness and simple courtesies still matter in Spain. A handshake on greeting and leaving is normal. You should always begin any conversation with *buenos días* (good morning) or *buenas tardes* (good afternoon/evening). It is customary to say hello when entering a shop. Always say *adiós*, or, at night, *buenas noches* when leaving. *Por favor* (please) should begin all requests.

	Valenciano	**Castilian**
good morning	*bon día*	**buenos días**
good afternoon/ good evening	*bona vesprada*	**buenas tardes**
good night	*bona nit*	**buenas noches**
please	*per favor*	**por favor**
thank you	*gràcies*	**gracias**
you're welcome	*de res*	**de nada**
goodbye	*adéu*	**adiós**

The *Berlitz Spanish Phrase Book & Dictionary* covers most situations you are likely to encounter during your travels in Spain, while the *Berlitz Spanish–English/English–Spanish Pocket Dictionary* contains some 12,500 entries, plus a menu-reader supplement.

Here are a few useful words that may come in handy:

yes	**sí**
no	**no**
excuse me	**perdone**
where?	**¿dónde?**
when?	**¿cuándo?**
how?	**¿cómo?**
who?	**¿quien?**
yesterday/today/tomorrow	**ayer/hoy/mañana**
day/week/month/year	**día/semana/mes/año**
left/right	**izquierda/derecha**
up/down	**arriba/abajo**
good/bad	**bueno/malo**
big/small	**grande/pequeño**
cheap/expensive	**barato/caro**
hot/cold	**caliente/frío**
old/new	**viejo/nuevo**
open/closed	**abierto/cerrado**
Waiter!/Waitress!	**¡Camarero!/¡Camarera!**
I'd like…	**Quisiera…**
How much is that?	**¿Cuánto es?**
What time is it?	**¿Qué hora es?**
Is there anyone here who speaks English?	**¿Hay alguien aquí que hable inglés?**
I don't understand.	**No entiendo.**
Do you speak English?	**¿Habla usted inglés?**
I don't speak Spanish.	**No hablo español.**

LOST PROPERTY

If you lose an item of value, report the loss to the Municipal Police or the Guardia Civíl (see POLICE). Be sure to ask for a copy of the police report, which you will need to make an insurance claim once you are home.

I've lost my wallet/handbag/ passport.	**He perdido mi cartera/bolso/ pasaporte.**

M

MAPS

Road maps are on sale at most petrol stations, bookshops and newsstands. Road and street signs often carry place names both in Castilian and *Valenciano* – a fact not reflected on every map.

a street plan of...	**un plano de la ciudad de...**
a road map of this region	**un mapa de carreteras de esta comarca**

MEDIA

Newspapers and magazines *(periódicos, revistas)*. In tourist towns you can buy most European and British newspapers on the day of publication, as well as the *International Herald Tribune*. Most glossy European and American magazines are available. The *Costa Blanca News* is the coast's oldest established English newspaper.

Radio and television *(radio, televisión)*. The BBC World Service and other international radio stations can be picked up on a short-wave radio. A number of local stations broadcast all or part of their output in English, notably REM FM which claims to be Spain's largest

English-language broadcasting network: tune to 92.7FM, or listen on <www.rem.fm>. English-language satellite television is widely available in hotels and English-run bars.

Have you any English-language newspapers/magazines?	**¿Tienen periódicos/revistas en inglés?**

MONEY

Currency. The euro (€) is the official currency used in Spain. Notes are denominated in 5, 10, 20, 50, 100, 200 and 500 euros; coins in 1 and 2 euros and 1, 2, 5, 10, 20 and 50 cents.

Banking hours. Monday–Friday 9am–2pm; some branches open on Saturday until 1pm. Outside these hours, currency can usually be changed at a *cambio* (bureau de change) or in your hotel. Always take your passport. You can also use ATMs *(cajeros automáticos)* to draw funds in euros against your bank account with a credit/debit card.

Credit cards. All the internationally recognised cards are accepted by hotels, restaurants and businesses in Spain.

Traveller's cheques. Most shops, hotels and travel agencies in tourist area accept traveller's cheques, although you're likely to get a better exchange rate at a national or regional bank.

I want to change some pounds/dollars.	**Quiero cambiar libras/ dólares.**
Do you accept traveller's cheques?	**¿Acepta usted cheques de viaje?**
Can I pay with this credit card?	**¿Puedo pagar con esta tarjeta de crédito?**

O

OPENING HOURS

Opening and closing times vary, but usual hours are 9.30am–1.30pm or 2pm and 4.30pm or 5pm–8pm.

Banks. Monday–Friday 9am–2pm; some branches open on Saturday until 1pm.

Bars and restaurants. Most restaurants open 1.30–4pm and 9pm–11pm, but in the resorts many bars open from noon or earlier until the small hours. Less formal restaurants open all day.

Post office. Monday–Friday 9am–1 or 2pm and 4 or 5pm–6 or 7pm, (but some only open in the morning 9am–2pm). Mornings only on Saturday.

Shops. Monday–Saturday 9am–1pm and 4–8pm.

Are you open tomorrow? **¿Está abierto mañana?**

P

PHOTOGRAPHY *(fotografía)*

There's tremendous scope for the keen photographer, but beware of the strong light. For good results don't shoot between 11am and 3pm unless there's light cloud to soften the sun.

All popular brands of memory card are available. Only a few shops now stock film. Shops in major resorts usually provide a reasonably priced and quick processing service for both film and disks.

It is forbidden to take photographs of any military bases, military or naval port areas, police, government or military personnel.

POLICE *(policía;* see also EMERGENCIES)

There are three police forces in Spain: the *Policía Municipal,* local units in a blue uniform; the *Policía Nacional,* a national anti-crime unit also in a blue uniform; and the *Guardia Civíl,* the national police force, in a green uniform. You can call on any of the three in an emergency.

Where's the nearest police station?	**¿Dónde está la comisaría más cercana?**

POST OFFICES *(correos)*

These are used for post and telegrams, not telephone calls. Stamps *(sellos)* are sold at any tobacconists (called *estancos*, but marked *tabacos)* and by most shops that also sell postcards. Post boxes are painted yellow and the opening marked *extranjero* is for overseas mail.

Poste restante. If you don't know in advance where you will be staying, you can still have mail forwarded to you addressed *poste restante (apartado de correos)* at whichever town is most convenient. When collecting it you must take your passport to the post office as identification.

Where is the (nearest) post office?	**¿Dónde está la oficina de correos (más cercana)?**
Have you received any mail for …?	**¿Ha recibido correo para…?**
A stamp for this letter/postcard, please.	**Por favor, un sello para esta carta/tarjeta.**
express (special delivery)	**urgente**
airmail	**vía aérea**
registered	**certificado**

PUBLIC HOLIDAYS *(fiestas)*

1 January	*Año Nuevo*	New Year's Day
6 January	*Epifanía*	Epiphany
1 May	*Día del Trabajo*	Labour Day
15 August	*Asunción*	Assumption
9 October	*Día de la Comunidad Valenciana*	
12 October	*Día de la Hispanidad*	Columbus Day
1 November	*Todos los Santos*	All Saints' Day
6 December	*Día de la Constitución Española*	Constitution Day
8 December	*Inmaculada Concepción*	Immaculate Conception
25 December	*Navidad*	Christmas Day

Movable dates:

March/April	*Jueves Santo*	Maundy Thursday
	Viernes Santo	Good Friday
May/June	*Corpus Christi*	Corpus Christi

PUBLIC TRANSPORT *(transporte público)*

Buses. There are bus services from Alicante bus station (tel: 965 130 700) to most towns in the province and cities further afield. Book your ticket from the relevant kiosk inside the hall. The various companies almost always put on sufficient buses to take waiting passengers, so make sure you get the right one; ie don't get on the first bus if your ticket says 'Autobús 2'. If you've got a ticket, you've got a bus.

Outside Alicante enquire about bus routes and times at the local bus terminal *(estación de autobuses)*, tourist office, travel agency or hotel. Most coastal routes are hourly and reasonably regular.

Taxis. Spain's taxi fares compare very favourably with those in the rest of Europe. If you are going outside the urban area where the meter operates, check the approximate fare *before* setting off. If you travel outside a town, you'll be charged the two-way trip unless there is a return fare. Except in Benidorm and Alicante, taxis tend to disappear around midnight, earlier out of season. By Spanish law taxis may only take four persons per vehicle (although some are willing to risk a fifth if it is a baby or child). A green light and/or a *libre* ('free') sign indicates a taxi is available.

Trains *(trenes)*. Spain's mainline train services are operated by RENFE (tel: 902 240 202; <www.renfe.es>) which has its Costa Blanca hub at Alicante. Trains are divided into *cercanías* (local mainly commuter services), *regionales* (connecting the towns in the Valencia region) and *grandes líneas*, fast, comfortable long-distance trains for which a seat reservation is essential. A narrow-gauge railway line runs from Alicante to Denia (tel: 900 720 472 or see <www.fgvalicante.com>), stopping frequently at points along the coast before moving inland after Altea. The whole journey takes just over two hours. An old-fashioned tourist train, the Limón Expres, runs services along the northern part of the line from Benidorm. Another narrow-gauge railway runs from Los Nietos on the Mar Menor into the city of Cartagena.

Ferries. Balearia (tel: 902 160 180; <www.balearia.net>) operates a ferry service between Denia, Ibiza and Mallorca.

When's the next bus to…?	**¿Cuándo sale el próximo autobús para…?**
single (one-way)	**ida**
return (round-trip)	**ida y vuelta**
When/Which is the best train to…?	**¿Cuándo/Cuál es el mejor tren para…?**
I'd like to make seat reservations.	**Quiero reservar asientos.**

R

RELIGION

The national religion is Roman Catholicism, but other denominations and faiths are represented. The Costa Blanca has a permanent English-speaking Protestant chaplain who functions in various churches and centres, mostly between Benidorm and Denia. The Evangelical Church also has a small but strong following; services, in Spanish, are held regularly. The Synagogue in Benidorm (Calle Berlín, Edificio Parque Loix) holds Sabbath services on Friday evenings. The *Costa Blanca News* carries details of religious services.

S

SIESTA

Although not everyone sleeps a siesta after lunch, they do take a long break from approximately 1.30 to 5pm.

T

TELEPHONES *(teléfono)*

You can make local, national and international calls from public phone booths *(cabinas)* in the streets, which operate with coins or cards. Phone cards *(tarjetas telefónicas)* can be purchased at tobacconists *(estancos)* or post offices. You can also make calls at public telephone centres called *locutorios*, where you call from a booth and pay at the desk afterwards. Calls from a hotel room are the most expensive option.

To make an international call dial **00** + country code + phone number, omitting the initial zero. The country code for the UK is **44**, for US and Canada **1**, for Australia **61** and for Ireland **353**.

The country code for Spain is **34**. The provincial area code is **96**, which must be included even for local numbers.

TIME DIFFERENCES

Spanish time coincides with most of Western Europe – Greenwich Mean Time (GMT) plus one hour. In spring, another hour is added (Daylight Saving Time).

New York	London	**Spain**	Jo'burg	Sydney	Auckland
6am	11am	**noon**	noon	8pm	10pm

TIPPING *(propinas)*

A service charge is normally included in hotel and restaurant bills, and tipping is not obligatory, though it is the normal practice to leave a little small change on a bar counter or restaurant table. If you want to tip a taxi driver, 5 percent will be enough, unless he or she has been especially helpful. A common Spanish way of tipping in all circumstances is to round up the bill to the nearest euro or so.

TOILETS

There are many expressions for toilets in Spanish: *aseos, servicios, WC, wáter* and *retretes.*

Where are the toilets?	**¿Dónde están los servicios?**

TOURIST INFORMATION *(oficina de turismo)*

Spanish National Tourist Offices are maintained throughout the world. See also <www.spain.info>.

Canada: 2 Bloor Street West, Suite 3402, Toronto, Ontario M4W 3E2, tel: (416) 961 3131, email: <toronto@tourspain.es>.

UK: 79 New Cavendish Street, 2nd floor, W1W 6XB, tel: 020 7486 8077, email: <londres@tourspain.es>, <www.tourspain.co.uk>.

US: Suite 915 East, 845 North Michigan Avenue, Chicago, IL 60611, tel: (312) 642 1992, email: <chicago@tourspain.es>.

8383 Wilshire Boulevard, Suite 960, Beverly Hills, CA 90211, tel: (323) 658 7195, email: <losangeles@tourspain.es>.
666 Fifth Avenue, New York, NY 10103, tel: (212) 265 8822, email: <nuevayork@tourspain.es>.
1395 Brickell Avenue, Miami, FL 33131, tel: (305) 358 1992, email: <miami@tourspain.es>.

These offices will readily supply you with a wide range of informative brochures and maps in English on the various towns and regions in Spain.

All cities and resorts in Spain have their own tourist information offices which will be delighted to provide you with information and brochures on local tourist attractions.

W

WATER *(agua)*

The rain in Spain doesn't fall much along the Costa Blanca, where tap water is a precious commodity. There are periodic droughts and occasionally shortages, causing problems that can prove a nuisance (water turned off at night, etc).

When Spaniards drink water, it is almost invariably bottled, not tap water. It is quite common to order water to be sent to one's room. If you're particularly sensitive to water while travelling, watch out, too, for the ice cubes in drinks.

WEBSITES AND INTERNET CAFÉS

Internet cafés are widespread. Check at the local tourist office for a list. You can expect to pay approximately €5 for an hour online.

Useful websites to help with the planning of your holiday include:
www.costablanca.org The official website for the Costa Blanca.
www.comunitatvalenciana.com The main regional website.
www.costamediterranea.com A commercial tourist website.
www.spain.info The official website for tourism in Spain.

Recommended Hotels

Spanish hotels are graded one to five stars depending upon facilities. Some establishments are classified as *hostales* (with one to three stars) and others *pensiones* – these are not necessarily less welcoming or less comfortable than a hotel of higher rank. The suffix *residencia* to a hotel or *hostal* means that there is no dining room, although breakfasts may still be served.

Costa Blanca's beach towns are popular with the tourist crowd, so if you are looking for more secluded accommodation, try staying at the less-developed towns such as Jávea, Calpe and Altea. During the high season (July and August) it is virtually impossible to find a hotel anywhere on the Costa Blanca without advance reservations.

All but the very cheapest hotels, hostels and *pensiones* accept credit cards. Establishments are open all year round unless otherwise stated. As a basic guide to room prices, the following price categories are for double occupancy during the mid-season.

€€€€	above 90 euros
€€€	60–90 euros
€€	40–60 euros
€	below 40 euros

AGUILAS

Al Sur €€€ *Torre de Cope 24, 30889 Calabardina, tel: 968 419 466, <www.halsur.com>*. Situated 10km (6 miles) north of Aguilas, this hotel has great views over Cabo Cope. Various sports are on offer, including sailing, canoeing, diving and cycling. 9 rooms.

ALICANTE

Abba Centrum €€€–€€€€ *Pintor Lorenzo, Casanova 31, tel: 965 130 440, <www.abbacentrumalicante.com>*. An ultra-modern hotel decorated with stainless steel, glass and shining marble floors and avant-garde furniture. The location is convenient for the bus station. Ask about special offers. 116 rooms.

Almirante €€–€€€ *Avenida de Niza 38, Playa San Juan, tel: 965 650 112, <www.hotelalmirante.com>*. On Playa de San Juan, 10km (6 miles) north of the city centre, with sea views from the bedrooms. Pool, restaurant, cafeteria, children's playground and parking. 68 rooms.

Hospes Amérigo Alicante €€€ *Rafael Altamira 7, tel: 965 146 570, <www.hospes.es>*. A beautiful spa-hotel housed in an old convent close to the harbour. Spa, fitness centre, massage/relaxation service. Great views of Santa Barbara castle from the bar. Excellent restaurant.

Les Monges Palace €€€ *San Agustín 4, tel: 965 215 046, <www.lesmonges.net>*. This historic city-centre building has been lovingly restored to make a comfortable, arty, small hotel with 18 rooms.

ALTEA

Altaya €€€ *Sant Pere 28, tel: 965 840 800, <www.hotelaltaya.com>*. Beach hotel close to the town centre, with bright and airy rooms; some have sea views. Good restaurant specialising in Valencian cuisine. Parking available. 24 rooms.

BENIDORM

Gran Hotel Bali €€€–€€€€ *Luis Prendes 4, tel: 966 815 200, <www.granhotelbali.com>*. This four-star hotel is the highest building in Spain and has amazing views of the Mediterranean from its bedrooms. Gym, health and fitness centre, pool, children's facilities, business centre, bars, shops. Disabled access. The hotel is 400m (400yds) from the sea and 2km (just over a mile) from the city centre.

BENISSA

Casa del Maco €€€–€€€€ *Pou Roig 15, tel: 965 732 842, <www.casadelmaco.com>*. A renovated 18th-century farmhouse surrounded by almond trees, vines and olive trees, near the Sierra de Bernia and Castell de Guadalest. There are only 6 bedrooms and all have been carefully furnished with antiques. Swimming pool. The paved terrace has views of Calpe's Peñón de Ifach.

BIAR

Mas Fontanelles €€€ *Carretera Biar-Bañeres (CV-804) km 4, tel: 686 426 126, <www.masfontanelles.com>.* In a peaceful setting in the Sierra de Fontanell, this hotel occupies a 200-year-old stone country house. Rooms are light and beautifully decorated.

BOCAIRENTE

L'Agora €€€ *Sor Piedad de la Cruz 3, tel: 962 355 039, <www.lagorahotel.com>.* A beautiful town hotel in a renovated art-nouveau building. The rooms are decorated in strikingly different styles – Thai, Chinese, African, Pakistani and so on. 8 rooms.

L'Estació €€€ *Parc de la Estació, tel: 962 350 000, <www.hotelestacio.com>.* An old railway station converted into a warm and cosy hotel. Bedrooms are light and one has disabled access. 14 rooms.

CALLOSA D'EN SARRIÀ

El Repos del Viatger €€ *Carrer Major 1, tel: 965 882 322, <www.casaruralelreposdelviatger.com>.* A bed-and-breakfast in the town centre, on the way up to the Sierra de Guadalest. The 5 bedrooms are decorated with local antiques.

CALPE

Marisol Park €€€ *Urbanización Marisol Park 1A, tel: 965 875 700, <www.marisolpark.com>.* Located in the Marisol Park estate, this hotel has three outdoor swimming pools, an indoor pool, terraces, a tropical garden and various sports facilities. Bedrooms are spacious and light, and decorated with modern furniture. All bedrooms have terraces and views of the sea and of the Peñón de Ifach.

EL CAMPELLO

Pueblo Acantilado €€€€ *Carretera N332 km 127, tel: 965 638 146, <www.h-puebloacantilado.com>.* Located on a cliff between

Alicante and Villajoyosa, a variety of luxury accommodation is available from single rooms to villas. The *suit royal*, on three levels, is considered one of the best hotel rooms available in Spain.

CASTELL DE CASTELLS

Casa Rural Pilar €€ *San José 2, tel: 965 518 157, <www.casapilar.com>*. A bed-and-breakfast in a 19th-century village house in the mountains behind the Costa Blanca. The seven bedrooms are decorated with local antiques and the dining room is in a vaulted cellar.

DENIA

Buenavista €€€ *Tossalet 82, tel: 965 787 995, <www.buenavista.com>*. This small hotel, just outside Denia, stands in a wooded estate surrounded by a garden of aromatic Mediterranean plants. Restaurant, swimming pool, sauna and gym. 17 rooms.

La Posada del Mar €€€€ *Plaza de les Drassanes, tel: 966 432 966, <www.laposadadelmar.com>*. A beautiful hotel in a historic 18th-century harbour building, at the foot of Denia castle and 300m (300yds) from the beach. 16 rooms, 9 junior suites.

GANDIA

La Falconera €€€€ *Cami Pinet 32, Marxuquera, tel: 962 868 315, <www.lafalconera.com>*. Located 10 minutes' away from Gandia's beaches, and facing La Falconera Mountain, this beautiful hotel with white walls and curvacious staircases is surrounded by a lovely garden planted with eucalyptus, palm trees and ancient pine trees. The suites have balconies with mountain views. It has its own vegetable garden, a terrace and swimming pool. 4 suites.

Molí el Canyisset €€€ *Carretera Font d'Encarros–Beniarjo, La Font d'en Carros, tel: 962 833 217, <www.hotelcanyisset.com>*. A rebuilt 17th-century rice mill with a tall chimney, 5km (3 miles) from Gandia's beaches. The rooms are beautifully decorated with antique and modern furniture. Restaurant and swimming pool. 16 rooms.

JÁTIVA

Huerto de la Virgen de Las Nieves €€€–€€€€ *Avenida de la Ribera 6, tel: 962 287 058, <www.huertodelavirgendelasnieves.com>.* This hotel is a converted 19th-century country house. The restaurant serves the two typical desserts of Játiva, *almoixávena* and *arnadi*. Swimming pool and garden. 6 rooms. Parking at extra charge.

Mont Sant €€€€ *Subida al Castillo, tel: 962 275 081, <www.montsant.com>.* A rural house, surrounded by gardens, built on the ruins of a monastery at the foot of the castle. It has been restored keeping the structure of the building while adding modern conveniences. The six rooms are individually decorated and have views over the city, the castle and the gardens. One room is a suite with its own swimming pool. In the gardens, there are 10 comfortable log cabins.

JÁVEA

Jávea €€–€€€ *Pío X 5, tel: 965 795 463, <www.hotel-javea.com>.* The prices of rooms in this modern hotel near Javea port vary according to the season but also according to their views – those with sea views are more expensive than interior ones – but all are light and decorated in minimalist white. The hotel can arrange scuba-diving courses, horse-riding lessons and golf for guests. 24 rooms.

El Rodat €€€€ *La Murciana 9, Carretera Cabo de la Nao s/n, Urbanización El Tosalet, tel: 966 470 710, <www.elrodat.com>.* A luxury country-house hotel with a beautiful garden and a swimming pool. Its 42 rooms include 4 suites and several holiday bungalows, each with its private garden. Restaurant, terrace and swimming pool.

LA MANGA DEL MAR MENOR

Villas La Manga €€€–€€€€ *Gran Vía km 3, La Manga del Mar Menor, tel: 968 145 222, <www.villaslamanga.es>.* A handsome building in pleasing contrast to the skyscraper hotels and apartments that make up much of La Manga. The restaurant offers both buffet and à la carte dining. Swimming pool. 60 'mini-suites'.

MURCIA (CITY)

Arco de San Juan €€€–€€€€ *Plaza de Ceballos 10, tel: 968 210 455, <www.arcosanjuan.com>*. A four-star hotel in Murcia's city centre, in a neo-classical 18th-century palace (Palacio del Conde de Floridablanca). It has a renowned restaurant and a cafeteria which stages exhibitions of local painters. Private parking is available.

El Churra €€–€€€ *Marques de los Vélez 12, tel: 968 238 400, <www.elchurra.net>*. A large, modern and functional hotel near the Plaza Circular, with large and comfortable bedrooms, business facilities and wireless internet access in all bedrooms. It has its own private parking (for a fee) and a cafeteria with a non-smoking area. The restaurant of the same name is in the street behind.

RUGAT

La Casa Vieja €€€ *Carrer del Forn 4, tel: 962 814 013, <www.lacasavieja.com>*. A hotel with five rooms and one suite, located in a peaceful village between Gandia and Albaida. The 450-year-old house has been lovingly restored, keeping the original arches, stones, beams and columns. It is decorated with antiques, family heirlooms, watercolour paintings, Persian carpets and pretty fabrics. There are no televisions in the hotel and calm is guaranteed.

SANTA POLA

Picola €–€€ *Alicante 66, tel: 965 411 868*. In Santa Pola's historic centre, near the bus station and a 10-minute walk from the beach, is this small *hostal* which has comfortable rooms, all with air-conditioning. The restaurant specialises in Valencian dishes.

TABARCA ISLAND

Casa del Gobernador €€€ *Arzola 2, Isla de Tabarca, tel: 965 960 886, <www.casadelgobernador.com>*. This small hotel, on the island of Tabarca, off the coast of Santa Pola, occupies the 18th-century governor's house. Sea views are guaranteed. 14 rooms.

TÁRBENA

Casa Lehmi €€€€ *El Buscarró 1, tel: 902 878 001, <www.casalehmi.com>*. Situated 20km (12 miles) inland from the coast at 420m (1,380ft) in a valley which forms part of a nature reserve, this hotel is in a restored country house. Swimming pool.

TORREVIEJA

Masa International €€€ *Avenida Alfredo Nobel 150, tel: 966 921 537, <www.hotelmasa.com>*. This lovely cliff-top hotel stands next to one of Torrevieja's 8th-century watchtowers at a convenient distance from the bustle of the town. Swimming pool, sauna and parking. Some rooms have views of the bay. 50 rooms.

VALENCIA

Ad Hoc €€€ *Boix 4, tel: 963 919 140, <www.adhochoteles.com>*. A charming hotel in a restored 19th-century mansion on the edge of the old town near the river. It has great character with its patio garden, exposed brickwork and beams. 28 rooms.

Antigua Morellana €€ *En Bou 2, tel: 963 915 773, <www.hostalam.com>*. A small 18th-century hotel in a little street between La Lonja and Plaza de la Reina. Good value. 18 rooms.

VILLAJOYOSA

El Almendral de Relleu €€€€ *Finca El Almendral, Partida Rural El Terme, Carretera CV-775 km 18, Relleu, tel: 659 164 965/659 165 085, <www.almendral.com>*. Remote, utterly peaceful place with few amusements laid on. It will be just you, 2,800 almond trees and uninterrupted views of the peaks. 6 rooms.

Las Puertas del Indiano €€€€ *Alicante 23, Relleu, tel: 966 856 326, <www.puertasindiano.com>*. This hotel-spa is in a village inland from Villajoyosa, near Sella and Orxeta. The terrace solarium has views of the castle. No children. 6 rooms.

Recommended Restaurants

Most of the restaurants listed below are those serving local cuisine but there are many good restaurants serving international cuisine – a few of which are mentioned.

It is advisable to book in advance for dinner at all establishments during high season. If you are on a budget, or just confused by the menu, choose the *menú del día* (daily menu), which is offered by most restaurants (at weekday lunchtimes in particular) and can often represent outstanding value.

Some restaurants close one day a week, and some open only for dinner, with seasonal variations.

The following price catagories are based on the approximate cost of dinner for two, not including drinks:

€€€	over 60 euros
€€	35–60 euros
€	below 35 euros

ALCOY

Lolo €€€ *Partida Rambla Alta, 98, tel: 965 547 373.* A very popular country restaurant in a former farmhouse with beautiful views of Alcoy, specialising in seasonal Mediterranean and mountain cuisine using fresh market produce. On the menu is a selection of 20 different rice dishes. Try the *habitas salteadas* (sautéed baby broad beans) or the home-made *croquetas*. Finish with the rich chocolate cake. The wine list features wines from Alicante and Valencia. Booking essential. Closed Mondays.

ALICANTE

Auberge de France €€€ *Flora de España 32, tel: 965 260 602.* This upmarket restaurant specialises in Mediterranean food as well as French cuisine. Try the delicious salad of green asparagus with duck and foie gras, or the artichoke filled with seafood. Closed Monday and the second half of October.

La Cantera €€€ *Avenida de Villajoyosa 6, tel: 965 236 606, <www.restaurantelacantera.com>*. A spacious seaside restaurant decorated in a minimalist style making maximum use of natural light. There are also two big terraces, one of them with lovely sea views. Closes Sunday evening and Monday.

Dársena €€€ *Marina Deportiva, Muelle 6, tel: 965 207 589, <www.darsena.com>*. An elegant restaurant on Alicante's seafront, with a nautical atmosphere and big windows offering beautiful views of both the port and the city. It serves Mediterranean cuisine and specialises in traditional rice dishes.

Jumillano €€€ *Cesar Elguezábal 62–64, tel: 965 212 964, <www.restaurantejumillano.com>*. This venerable old restaurant with a bullfighting atmosphere in the heart of Alicante serves fish and traditional regional dishes. Oxtail stew is the speciality of the house. Closed Sunday in summer.

Monastrell €€€ *San Fernando 10, tel: 965 200 635, <www.monastrell.com>*. An avant-garde restaurant with a decoration scheme based on straight lines, glass, granite, wood and stainless steel. Chef Maria José San Román is known for her creative use of saffron. Choose from the à la carte menu, or the fixed-price gastronomic or saffron menus. Closed Sunday evening and Monday.

Nou Manolin €€ *Villegas 3, tel: 965 200 368, <www.noumanolin.com>*. This well-established restaurant specialises in ultra-fresh produce – the fish arrives alive every morning from the harbour. It's a good place to sample traditional rice dishes such as *arroz al horno* (baked savoury rice).

ALMORADI

El Cruce €€€ *Camino de Catral 156, tel: 965 700 356*. This traditional restaurant between Orihuela and the coast is a good find for vegetarians as the vegetables come straight from the farm. Artichokes are a speciality. It also serves *pava borracha*, a turkey stew typical of the area. Closed on Sunday evenings, Monday and August.

ALTEA

Casa Labarta €€€€ *Conde de Altea 30, tel: 965 845 112, <www.casalabarta.com>*. A bar and restaurant on Altea's seafront with a terrace overlooking the sea. It serves paella and other traditional rice dishes as well as a selection of tapas, including squid in tomato sauce, fried aubergines, fish kebabs and home-made desserts.

Oustau de Altea €€€ *Mayor 5, tel: 965 842 078, <www.oustau.com>*. Located in the old part of town, inside a renovated 200-year-old convent, this restaurant specialises in French cuisine. The most popular dish is the unusual, but delicious, sirloin steak with strawberry sauce. Closed Monday in winter.

Racó de Toni €€ *Carrer La Mar 127, tel: 965 841 763*. A traditional family-run mesón offering a good selection of tapas and several regional staples but also some more creative dishes. The desserts are home-made. Closed one week in September, and November.

BENIDORM

Aitona €€ *Ruzafa 2, Rincón de Loix, tel: 965 853 010*. Don't be put off by the gigantic paella-pan signboard outside. Locals rate this city-centre restaurant for its various regional rice dishes – including such ingredients as squid and cauliflower – and wood-grilled meats.

I Fratelli €€€ *Doctor Orts Llorca 2, tel: 965 853 979*. Gourmet restaurant with art deco decoration, serving splendid Italian cuisine and other international dishes. Specialities include foie gras *(higado de oca)*, buffalo mozzarella in salad and apple and pear strudel with vanilla ice cream. Closed in November.

La Palmera €€ *Avenida Doctor Severo Ochoa 48, Rincón de Loix, tel: 965 853 282*. A family-run restaurant specialising in seafood and fish dishes backed up by a good wine selection. Try the *fideuá con rape y almejas* (noodles with monkfish and clams) or *calderos marineros* (fish stews). For dessert there are home-made ice creams and chocolate tart. Closed Sunday evening and Monday.

Ulía €€€ *Avenida Vicent Llorca Alos, Rincón de Loix, tel: 966 804 059.* The terrace of this beach restaurant is one of the best places to eat Valencian rice dishes such as paella, *arroz negro* (black rice with squid ink) or *arroz a banda* (rice cooked in fish stock). If you don't want to order rice, try the *caldero de bogavante* (fish stew). Closed Sunday evening and Monday.

BENIMANTELL (NEAR GUADALEST)

L'Obrer €€ *Carretera Alcoy 25, tel: 965 885 088.* Grilled and roast meats are on the menu of this mountain restaurant, which is one of the favourite haunts of the local expatriate community. Best of all are the thick mountain stews that are typical of the Guadalest valley. Open for lunch only. Closed Friday.

Trestellador €€ *Partida Trestellador 101, tel: 965 885 221, <www.hostaltrestellador.com>.* Traditional cooking is served in this spacious restaurant which enjoys great views of the Guadalest valley and of the hills descending towards the coast. Try mountain dishes such as olleta de blat (a stew of meat and wheat), *cordero al horno* (roast lamb) and *pilotes* (meat balls).

BENISSA

Casa Cantó €€€ *País Valenciano 237, tel: 965 730 629.* A traditional Mediterranean restaurant with magnificent views that specialises in seafood and paella dishes. Try the *arroz Ximo*, the house-style rice. Closed Sunday and all November.

Casa del Maco €€€ *Pou Roig-Lleus, tel: 965 732 842, <www.casadelmaco.com>.* This restaurant, in an 18th-century renovated farmhouse, offers a wonderful blend of French and international cuisine in very elegant surroundings.

Al Zaraq €€€ *Partida Benimarraig 79 (between Benissa and Calpe), tel: 965 731 615, <www.alzaraq.net>.* Oriental-style restaurant with views over Calpe bay and the Peñón de Ifach, serving Lebanese cuisine and excellent traditional dishes prepared to perfection.

BIAR

Mas Fontanelles €€ *Carretera Biar–Bañeres km 4, tel: 686 426 126.* An advance reservation is essential at this country-house hotel and restaurant, which is located in the Sierra de Fontanell. Home cooking is offered, combining Valencian and French influences, with the menu varying according to seasonal availability.

CALPE

Puerto Blanco €€€ *Urbanización La Canuta Baja 35b, tel: 965 830 977, <www.puerto-blanco.com>.* Located in the small harbour of La Canuta, this restaurant has a choice of dining rooms and a lovely terrace. Try their house speciality: *langostinos* with spicy Thai sauce. Open for dinner only during the week but for lunch also at weekends.

Los Zapatos €€ *Santa Maria 7, tel: 965 831 507, <www.loszapatos.com>.* A small restaurant serving French cuisine with oriental touches. It has regular painting exhibitions and live concerts of jazz, blues, classical music and flamenco. Special Sunday lunches are served. Closed Tuesday and Wednesday.

CARTAGENA

La Cocina de Alfonso €€–€€€ *Avenida Alfonso XIII 40, tel: 968 320 036.* One of the restaurants of the Hotel Alfonso XIII offering an excellent range of culinary styles, from traditional Murcian dishes to French and Japanese cuisine. Closed Sunday and August.

DENIA

El Asador del Puerto €€€ *Plaza del Raset 10–11, tel: 966 423 482.* Superb restaurant by the sea where you can eat Castilian and Mediterranean food and meats roasted in a wood-fired oven in elegant surroundings.

El Poblet €€€ *Urbanización El Poblet 43, Carretera Les Marines, tel: 965 787 662.* El Poblet is considered to be one of the very best restaurants in the Valencian region for its creative adaptation of Mediterreanean cuisine. Sampler menu *(menú de degustación)* available. Closed Sunday night, Monday, late February–mid-March and late November.

El Raset €€€ *Bellavista 7, tel: 965 785 040.* This is a pleasantly swish restaurant that attracts a loyal local clientele and is excellent for fish, seafood and rice dishes. Sampler menu *(menú de degustación)* available.

ELCHE

Els Capellans €€€ *Porta de la Morera 14, tel: 966 610 011.* Situated in Elche's famous palm grove, the restaurant of the Huerto del Cura serves traditional rice dishes with a Mediterranean flavour as well as more eclectic dishes. The service is excellent, as is the presentation.

El Granaino €€€ *José María Buch 40, tel: 965 664 080, <www.mesongranaino.com>.* Classy, family-owned restaurant close to the centre of Elche with an Andalusian atmosphere and popular with visiting celebrities. It serves traditional Spanish Mediterranean cuisine with an accent on the flavours of the south. Closed for two weeks in August.

GANDIA

La Casona €€€ *Irlanda (Urbanización San Nicolás between Gandía and its beach), tel: 962 845 959, <www.restaurantelacasona.es>.* A wide selection of starters precede a main-course menu that focuses on fish, meat and rice dishes, all accompanied by the fresh vegetables of the season. The desserts are home-made. There is a garden with outdoor tables.

JÁVEA

Amarre 152 €€ *La Marina, Arenal, Port de la Fontana, tel: 965 790 629.* Modern-style restaurant serving authentic traditional

Mediterranean food, particularly fish and rice dishes. If you don't feel like rice try the *cordero guisado a la antigua con patatas a lo pobre* (lamb stew with potatoes).

LA MANGA DEL MAR MENOR

Miramar €–€€ *Paseo del Puerto 14, Cabo de Palos, tel: 968 563 033*. Next to the fishing harbour at the end of La Manga, with views of the sea, this restaurant inevitably concentrates on fish and seafood. Closed Tuesday. Booking recommended.

MURCIA

Arco de San Juan €€–€€€ *Plaza de Ceballos 10, tel: 968 210 455, <www.arcosanjuan.com>*. The elegant restaurant of the Hotel Arco de San Juan offers sophisticated Murcian cuisine and international dishes. Closed weekends.

Palacete Rural la Seda €€€ *Vereda del Catalán, Santa Cruz (8km from Murcia), tel: 968 870 848, <www.palacetelaseda.com>*. A renovated 17th-century country house in the middle of the Murcian farmbelt. It is decorated with antiques and local arts and crafts. The menu is strong on Murcian cuisine.

PUERTO DE MAZARRON

Miramar €€ *Carretera Playa de la Isla 9, tel: 968 594 050, <www.restaurante-miramar.com>*. A fish and seafood restaurant located on the beach with sea views to enjoy as you dine. For the full works, order the *menú de degustación* (a taster menu of the house specialities), but there are cheaper options, including tapas. Closed Monday.

SANTA POLA

Patilla €€ *Elche 29, tel: 965 411 015*. Excellent seafood restaurant decorated in a nautical style and serving traditional rice dishes and fish fresh from the bay.

TORREVIEJA

La Fina Boca €€ *Avenida Alfred Nobel 155, tel: 966 923 385, <www.finaboca.com>*. This cosy, award-winning restaurant serves dishes deriving from 25 countries including France, Australia, India, Thailand and New Zealand. Open for dinner daily, but also for Sunday lunch.

VALENCIA

L'Estimat €€–€€€ *Paseo Neptuno 16, Playa de las Arenas, tel: 963 711 018, <www.lestimat.com>*. An institution on the Valencia beach that has been serving regional rice dishes, fresh fish and seafood since 1927. A very good place to eat paella or lesser known but equally delicious dishes such as *arroz a banda* (cooked in fish stock), *arroz al horno* (baked rice) or *arroz negro* (cooked in cuttlefish ink).

La Pepica €€–€€€ *Paseo Neptuno 2, 6 and 8, tel: 963 710 366, <www.lapepica.com>*. A classic Valencian restaurant founded in 1898 and visited by Hemingway and other writers, as well as bullfighters, artists and assorted VIPs. It is on a street along the beach which is lined with paella restaurants – some cheaper, where, arguably, you can eat just as well.

La Riua €€ *Calle de la Mar 27, tel: 963 914 571, <www.lariua.com>*. This family-run restaurant in the city centre offers a choice of typical Valencian cuisine, including rice and shellfish. It is acclaimed for its paella and other rice dishes, and for its *fideuá* (similar to paella but made with noodles).

VILLAJOYOSA

Hogar del Pescador €€ *Avenida País Valencia 33, tel: 965 890 021, <www.hogardelpescador.com>*. This family-run restaurant is situated on the main road through town. It has been serving fish, seafood and rice dishes for more than fifty years and its reputation is still going strong.

INDEX

Costa Blanca

Tenth Edition 2008

Written by David Henderson
Revised by Nick Inman
Edited by Alex Knights
Series Editor: Tony Halliday

Printed in Singapore by Insight Print Services (Pte) Ltd, 38 Joo Koon Road, Singapore 628990. Tel: (65) 6865-1600. Fax: (65) 6861-6438

Photography credits
All photography by Gregory Wrona/APA except 13, 45 Berlitz; 15 AKG-images London; 16 Instituto Geografico Nacional; 18 Archivo Iconografico, SA/Corbis; 20 Phillip/Fox Photos/ Getty Images; 22 David Tomlinson/Pictures Colour Library; 27 Andrew Critchell/Alamy; 28 Jose Fuste Raga/Corbis; 30 fotolincs/Alamy; 69 Guenter Fischer/Alamy; 80 Neil Buchan-Grant/ APA; 82 Caroline Commins/Alamy; 89 AM Corporation/Alamy; 99 Jon Santa Cruz/APA.

Cover picture: Reinhard Schmid/4Corners Images

Contact us

At Berlitz we strive to keep our guides as accurate and up to date as possible, but if you find anything that has changed, or if you have any suggestions on ways to improve this guide, then we would be delighted to hear from you.

Berlitz Publishing, PO Box 7910,
London SE1 1WE, England.
fax: (44) 20 7403 0290
email: berlitz@apaguide.co.uk
www.berlitzpublishing.com